Home Office Research Study 262

Drunk and disorderly: a qualitative study of binge drinking among 18- to 24-year-olds

Renuka Engineer, Annabelle Phillips, Julian Thompson and Jonathan Nicholls

The views expressed in this report are those of the authors, not necessarily those of the Home Office (nor do they reflect Government policy).

Home Office Research, Development and Statistics Directorate
February 2003

Home Office Research Studies

The Home Office Research Studies are reports on research undertaken by or on behalf of the Home Office. They cover the range of subjects for which the Home Secretary has responsibility. Other publications produced by the Research, Development and Statistics Directorate include Findings, Statistical Bulletins and Statistical Papers.

The Research, Development and Statistics Directorate

RDS is part of the Home Office. The Home Office's purpose is to build a safe, just and tolerant society in which the rights and responsibilities of individuals, families and communities are properly balanced and the protection and security of the public are maintained.

RDS is also part of National Statistics (NS). One of the aims of NS is to inform Parliament and the citizen about the state of the nation and provide a window on the work and performance of government, allowing the impact of government policies and actions to be assessed.

Therefore –

Research Development and Statistics Directorate exists to improve policy making, decision taking and practice in support of the Home Office purpose and aims, to provide the public and Parliament with information necessary for informed debate and to publish information for future use.

First published 2003

Application for reproduction should be made to the Communications and Development Unit, Room 201, Home Office, 50 Queen Anne's Gate, London SW1H 9AT.

© Crown copyright 2003   ISBN 1 84082 967 2

ISSN 0072 6435

Foreword

It is widely believed that there is a link between alcohol consumption and criminal and disorderly behaviour, especially in the young adult population. However, relatively little is known about the social context of such behaviour. This report uses focus groups to explore this issue, especially young adults' perceptions and experiences of, and motivations for, binge drinking.

The research focuses on the role of binge drinking within the night-time economy and concludes by suggesting ways in which a night out drinking could be made a safer and less threatening experience.

Four key elements that contribute to the relationship between binge drinking and disorder were identified: attitudes and motivations towards binge drinking; social and peer group norms; the effects of binge drinking on mood and behaviour and the drinking environment. Addressing some of the risk factors within each of these categories would seem a sensible approach to tackling the problem of alcohol-related crime and disorder.

TOM BUCKE
Drugs and Alcohol Research Programme
Research, Development and Statistics Directorate

Acknowledgments

The authors would like to thank Terry Honess (City University) and Professor Jim Orford (University of Birmingham) for acting as independent assessors for the report.

Many thanks are also due to the people who participated in this research, and to Anna Richardson and Tracey Budd of the Home Office Drugs and Alcohol Research Unit for their support and encouragement throughout the project.

Renuka Engineer is a Researcher at the MORI Social Research Institute.

Annabelle Phillips and Julian Thompson are both Senior Researchers at the MORI Social Research Institute.

Jonathan Nicholls is a Research Team Manager at the MORI Social Research Institute.

Recruitment for this study was carried out by MORI, and all group discussions were moderated by one of the four authors.

Contents

Summary

This report presents the findings from a qualitative study exploring the social context of binge drinking[1] among young adults aged from 18 to 24 years. The study examines young people's experiences of crime, disorder and risk-taking in the night-time economy, and explores ways in which drinking patterns, attitudes to drinking alcohol and the effects of binge drinking were related to these experiences. The research aims to provide an evidence base for the development of policies to reduce alcohol-related crime, disorder and violence, and public drunkenness.

The research consisted of 16 focus group discussions with young people, conducted across 8 locations in England and Wales. All of these young people had regular experience of binge drinking, and many reported behaving in ways associated with alcohol-related crime and disorder while out drinking.

The research identified four key elements of the social context that are relevant to the relationship between binge drinking and disorder: *attitudes and motivations* towards binge drinking, *social and peer group norms*, the *effects of binge drinking* on mood and behaviour, and the *drinking environment*. Key 'risk factors' were identified in each area. The research concluded that where these are present, and particularly when they interact, the likelihood of disorderly outcomes and risk-taking is increased. The report's conclusion illustrates and explains these integral relationships.

Implications of the research

Young binge drinkers enjoy drinking alcohol and being drunk. Few feel that their drinking habits are something that they should change, even when they have been involved in various forms of risk or disorder as a consequence. Indeed, episodes of risk and disorder are often viewed as part of the excitement of getting drunk with friends.

Getting drunk is an integral part of the social scene for these young people, although comments made by some about how their drinking habits have changed over the years suggest that they are likely to 'calm down' to some extent as they grow older and take on new responsibilities. For this reason, young people are unlikely to consider their drinking as a problem unless something quite serious happens to them while they are drunk. This means it may be difficult to reduce public drunkenness by changing the *attitudes* of the current

---

1   For the definition of binge drinking used in this study see Chapter 1, pp. 3-4, and Appendix A.

generation of young adults, although responsible serving practices may reduce more extreme consumption patterns. There may be more scope for having an impact on the behaviours that *surround* binge drinking, and so reducing the 'social harms' associated with binge drinking. This could involve measures to target the risk behaviours that the research has identified, e.g. young people aggravating strangers or using unlicensed minicabs.

The *drinking environment* can be as strong an influence on risk and offending in the night-time economy as individual attitudes, and young people believe that policies aimed at changing this environment are the most effective way to curb alcohol-related disorder. There is widespread support for extended licensing laws and a greater range of late-night venues to calm down the night-time economy, by slowing the pace of drinking and reducing the crowds of drinkers who are all on the move at the same time. There is also support for practical measures to ensure drinkers' safety, such as late-night transport, more targeted policing and the use of plastic glasses and bottles in pubs and clubs.

Advertising campaigns may have less of an impact, as young people are reluctant to change their levels of drinking and the attitudes associated with these. However, the behaviours that are common on a night out suggest there is a role for 'safer drinking' promotions that aim to alter the behaviour *around* binge drinking, by raising young people's awareness of the risks attached to certain situations. In this way, young people may be encouraged to take practical action to ensure their safety themselves, for example by arranging transport home in advance. This could involve messages conveyed either within the drinking environment (e.g. pub toilets), or outside of it (e.g. through broadcast media or in schools).

Despite their fervour for getting drunk, young people are aware that alcohol is a powerful drug that can have unpleasant consequences, and communications which highlight this fact are likely to stick in their minds if the messages are strong enough. While this is unlikely to change the amount that they drink on their next big night out, it may have a long-term influence on their overall perceptions of the risks associated with alcohol, and the choices they make before and after the pub or club.

Key findings – experience of risk and disorder

- Few young people saw themselves as being 'at risk' when they got drunk, particularly as only a small minority had been the victim of what they considered to be 'serious' offences. Nonetheless, they reported a range of risk-taking behaviours, including walking home alone, getting into cars or going home with strangers, using unlicensed mini-cabs and having unprotected sex. These risks were generally viewed as being more of a concern for young women.

● Risks were described as being taken for two reasons: from perceived necessity, and from alcohol making people more reckless, overconfident or determined to do as they pleased. However, several young people said that they preferred not to think about their night out in terms of risk, as this could interfere with their freedom and independence.

● Drunken fighting was seen as a 'fact of life' by most young people. They felt that confrontations were difficult to avoid when people were drunk and determined to fight. Many said that fights were caused more by personality than alcohol, while some blamed drunken violence on particular social groups. However, those who had been in fights themselves admitted that alcohol had influenced their judgements by making them feel more aggressive, reckless or over-confident than usual. Several young people associated particular drinks with aggression.

● Fights were often sparked when young people perceived a need to 'stand up' for themselves or for a friend or partner, while a few had friends who goaded them into fighting. In some cases fights were prompted by false or exaggerated perceptions of aggression or disrespect from other people. Fights were seen as more common on the streets after closing time, in known 'trouble spots' and in crowded venues.

● Many young people had committed drunken 'pranks', such as climbing buildings, or stopping traffic by moving 'street furniture'. They usually perceived these pranks as harmless fun, although they were more worried by the ones that had put them in physical danger. Alcohol was seen as the cause of these pranks, as it made them more reckless, impulsive or open to suggestion. Being 'egged on' by friends was frequently a factor.

● A few had been the victim of an offence because of a risk they took while drunk; incidents included being sexually assaulted in an unlicensed cab or after going to a stranger's house. The majority of young people who took risks while drunk had not had these kinds of experiences. Alcohol was seen as making people more vulnerable to attack, as it encourages incautious behaviour, blurs judgement and makes people appear as an easy target.

- Where people had been beaten up in fights, the distinction between offender and victim was often unclear. This reflects a key finding of the research; that the boundaries between 'risking', 'offending' and becoming a 'victim' while drunk are easily crossed. The majority of the young people had experienced more than one of these things while drinking, and many all three. Furthermore, there were cases in which one incident combined elements of all three categories of experience – particularly in the case of fights.

- Some of the young people used illegal drugs while out drinking, although other users were cautious about mixing drugs with drink. Those who were more relaxed about mixing said that using hard drugs such as Ecstasy, cocaine or amphetamines allowed them to keep drinking for longer, intensifying the 'high' associated with both kinds of substance. Some drug users compared drugs favourably with alcohol in terms of their effects, saying that they were less likely to cause aggression or affect a person's control of their own behaviour.

- Ways of avoiding trouble suggested by young people included pre-arranging taxis home, avoiding known 'trouble spots' and not wandering off alone when drunk.

Key findings – social context and risk factors

Key risk factors relating to young people's attitudes and motivations towards binge drinking were: *a desire to push the limits* and *difficulty judging the limits* with regard to alcohol consumption, an attitude among some that it was *fun to lose control*, the association of binge drinking with *personal freedom or escape*, and, in some instances, drinking to *relieve stress or anger*.

- Young people displayed a desire to 'push the limits' on a 'big night out'. These nights involve deliberately drinking with the intention of getting drunk, and the young people described mixing different drinks or drinking quickly in order to accelerate the process.

- While some young people anticipated or planned their 'big nights out', many described situations where a 'social drink' had turned unexpectedly into a drunken evening. The majority described finding it difficult to judge their limits and to slow down once the drinking session is underway, and the effects of drunkenness start becoming apparent.

- While many young people were concerned by the prospect of getting ill, losing their memory, or behaving out of character as a result of drinking, a significant minority saw these extremes as 'part of the fun' – an attitude that appears to have a correlation with, and may encourage, disorderly behaviour.

- Drinking was often linked to personal freedom and independence, and a desire to 'escape' from the concerns of day-to-day existence for a while. These attitudes encouraged some people to behave less responsibly than they would otherwise, or made them less likely to consider the consequences of their actions – for example, some young women chose to walk home alone rather than compromise their independence.

- While 'escapist' attitudes were common, drinking deliberately to relieve stress or anger was identified as a 'bad' motivation by some young people. They felt that alcohol was likely to exaggerate negative moods, making confrontations more likely. However, this awareness did not necessarily affect their actual behaviour.

Key risk factors relating to **social and peer group norms** were: *friends who encourage extreme behaviour*, the belief that *drunkenness is an acceptable excuse* for anti-social or reckless actions, *group overconfidence*, a perceived obligation to *stand up for friends or self*, and *tensions or prejudice between different social groups*.

- Peer group norms played a role in young people's perceptions of binge drinking as the 'done thing', and can influence young people's behaviour while drunk as well as their drinking patterns. Some described behaving or drinking quite differently when they were out with different groups of friends, or in a single-sex group rather than a mixed group. Some said their friends encouraged excessive drinking, fighting or dangerous pranks. Another justification given for misbehaviour was the attitude among some young people that *drunkenness is an acceptable excuse* that mitigates an individual's responsibility for their actions.

- Young people were likely to feel safe so long as they were with their friends, with several saying they would rely on friends to prevent them from doing something foolish. A few stressed the importance of having friends to 'back them up' in a confrontational situation. The fact that friends often all get very drunk together, and in some cases 'egg on' fighting or pranks, suggests that friends may provide a false sense of security in some cases.

- Fights were often sparked when young people perceived a need to 'stand up' for themselves or for a friend or partner. Many young people were very alert to the possibility of confrontation, with some even prepared to pre-empt fights from a perceived necessity to avoid being victimised. A few had a strong sense of their own 'personal space', which made them easily provoked in a crowded environment.

- Wider social identities were also viewed as relevant. Young drinkers' perceptions of each other were often affected by the fashion styles they adopted or the social groups they belonged to, a factor which could influence expectations about where to expect trouble and who to expect it from. This factor may aggravate confrontational situations.

Key risk factors relating to the **effects of binge drinking** on mood and behaviour were: *overconfidence, recklessness/impulsiveness, aggression, lack of awareness* of what is going on, *loss of control* and alcohol *blurring judgement.*

- The positive effects of alcohol were described as increased confidence, friendliness, a feeling of invulnerability and a desire to live for the moment. Young people were less likely to worry about how they looked or what was going on around them while they were drunk. However, a 'flip side' to these effects was also recognised; young people became *too* confident or carefree, misjudged what was going on around them, and were reckless about what they did or said in situations where they should have been more cautious. Some young people of both sexes related alcohol to feelings of aggression, particularly in relation to particular types of drink.

- The effects of drunkenness on mood and behaviour help to explain *why* binge drinking makes risk-taking and anti-social behaviour more likely among young people. They described being more inclined to act on impulse, thinking less about the consequences of their actions, and losing their tempers more easily when they were drunk.

Key risk factors relating to **the drinking environment** are: *restricted licensing laws, known 'trouble spots', crowded venues, irresponsible pub/club policy, lack of late-night transport, poor town centre layouts,* and, in smaller towns, *lack of late-night venues.*

- Trouble on a night out was associated with the fact that large numbers of young people were brought together, moving around in a relatively small space. Restricted licensing laws were seen as adding to the problems, by moving everybody outside at the same time. Problems after closing time were exacerbated by poor town centre layouts and lack of public transport or taxis – e.g. large numbers of people in a hurry to move on congregating on one taxi rank and arguing over taxis. In smaller towns, the lack of places to go after 11 p.m. was also criticised.

- Problems inside venues were often blamed on irresponsible pub/club policy, e.g. allowing overcrowding, letting in trouble-makers and serving people who had already had far too much to drink. The key role of bouncers in defusing violent situations was recognised, with many young people arguing that they made things worse by being unfair or aggressive. In addition to this, young people identified certain venues and parts of town as 'trouble spots', with an established pattern of violent incidents that they feel need to be addressed.

Key findings - interventions and messages

- Young people were generally in favour of changing the licensing laws to extend drinking hours. It was felt that this would allow people to leave venues 'in their own time' rather than all at once, making clashes between drunk people in town centres less likely. It was also felt that early closing times encouraged people to lose control by drinking too much too quickly. A few suggested that there should be a greater range of places for young people to go to late at night; for example, quiet places where drinkers could 'chill out' in addition to noisy night-clubs.

- Many were in favour of increasing the police presence outside pubs and clubs, particularly those known as 'trouble spots', although a few felt this might antagonise people. Young people also felt that both police and bouncers could do more to intervene in fight situations, and co-operate more effectively. Some favoured the use of plastic glasses in pubs and clubs to lessen the risk of injury. Provision of late-night public transport was seen as a key issue in certain areas.

- Young people felt they would be inclined to ignore 'safer drinking' campaigns, and that people only learned to be careful from personal experience. Some perceived these sorts of campaigns as 'lectures'. However, it was felt that 'shock' advertising had the potential to make an impression; for example, showing pictures of drunken injuries and diseased livers. Although such campaigns were seen as unlikely to change their drinking behaviour in the short term, it was felt they might raise their overall awareness of the risks associated with binge drinking.

Background & objectives

Alcohol use is an accepted part of social interaction in our culture, and the majority of adults in England and Wales drink alcohol regularly. Misuse of alcohol, however, can result in problems for the individual and society as a whole. Research shows that harmful patterns of drinking are associated with physical and mental health problems, accidents and crime and disorder. In response to these concerns, the Government is committed to developing a comprehensive National Alcohol Strategy by 2004.

A key objective for the Home Office is to maintain public safety and good order, as set out in the Home Office business plan 2001-2002. The Home Office Action Plan, 'Tackling alcohol-related crime, disorder and nuisance', sets out priorities for addressing levels of alcohol-related crime and disorder. The three key objectives of the Action Plan are:

- to reduce the problems arising from underage drinking;
- to reduce public drunkenness, and associated criminal and disorderly behaviour; and
- to prevent alcohol related violence[1].

This study was designed to inform policies addressing the latter two objectives[2]. The research focuses on 'binge drinking' among young people aged from 18 to 24, and provides an evidence base for the Home Office as it develops its Action Plan and for local services who are trying to target interventions at young people. In addition it contributes to the development of the National Alcohol Harm Reduction Strategy.

The report presents an analysis of sixteen 'focus group' discussions conducted with young adult binge drinkers. The discussions explored:

- young adults' drinking habits, particularly those leading to greater degrees of drunkenness, exploring their motivations for, and attitudes towards, getting drunk
- the social context surrounding drinking behaviour;
- the effects and consequences of binge drinking;
- disorderly behaviour and risk-taking while drunk, with a particular emphasis on how these situations arise and the role that alcohol has to play in such situations;

---

1   A full copy of the Action Plan can be downloaded from the Home Office website: www.homeoffice.gov.uk
2   Underage drinking is not explored in this report. For an exploration of the social context of underage drinking see Honess *et al.*, (2000).

- the interventions and messages that young people feel would, or would not, be effective in trying to encourage sensible drinking practices and reduce the social harms associated with binge drinking; and
- the links between binge drinking and illegal drug use.

The report is complemented by Home Office Research Study *Alcohol, Crime and Disorder; a study of young adults* (Richardson and Budd, 2003) which reports the results of secondary analysis of the 1998/1999 Youth Lifestyle Survey focusing on the links between binge drinking and criminal and disorderly behaviour among young adults

Structure of the report

The remainder of this chapter gives some further information about the study, and places it in the context of the existing research evidence. Following from this:

- *Chapter 2* examines the young people's drinking habits and attitudes towards drinking, including frequency of getting drunk, motivations for getting drunk, and associations with illegal drug use.
- *Chapter 3* explores the social context of binge drinking among young adults, including peer group influence, the drinking environment, and identification with broader social groups and the norms of 'British culture'.
- *Chapter 4* provides an overview of the effects of binge drinking on the young people's mood, behaviour and judgement, and a context for understanding the role these play in their risk-taking and disorderly behaviour.
- *Chapter 5* looks in depth at the young people's experiences of risk and disorder in the night-time economy, and examines the part played by the factors explored in Chapters 2 to 4 in these experiences. Subjects discussed include safety risks, sexual risks, fighting, drunken pranks, experiences as a victim and strategies for avoiding trouble.
- *Chapter 6* examines the young people's views on policies that aim to tackle alcohol-related crime and disorder, including interventions that change the drinking environment and advertising campaigns that highlight the risks and promote sensible drinking behaviour.
- *Chapter 7* presents a model for understanding the findings, identifying the 'risk factors' that interact to make risk-taking and disorderly behaviour more likely, and exploring how these relate to different aspects of the social context of binge drinking.

Understanding binge drinking

A 'binge' can be understood as a pattern of drinking that involves high consumption levels over a short time period. There has been a growing focus on 'binge' drinking in the field of alcohol studies in recent years, reflecting evidence which suggests that intermittent, high consumption drinking patterns are associated with certain health and social harms (see for example Moore *et al.*, 1994; Harnett *et al.*, 2000). For this reason, 'binge' drinking has also been termed 'Risky single-occasion drinking', or RSOD. 'Sessional' and 'episodic' drinking are also terms which have been utilised in the research literature (Murgraff *et al.*, 1999).

The 1995 Department of Health report *Sensible Drinking* recommended daily guidelines for the maximum number of units to be consumed[3]. This reflects concern that drinking within weekly consumption limits could mask short-term episodes of excessive drinking and intoxication, which may be strongly related to medical and social harms.

Defining binge drinking

Although there is widespread agreement among researchers and policymakers that binge drinking is an important issue, there is no universally agreed definition of binge drinking or standard way of measuring its occurrence (Murgraff *et al.*, 1999).

One definition that has been frequently used in the UK is men drinking at least eight units, or women drinking at least six units, on at least one day in the past week. This definition has been utilised in several nationally representative, government funded surveys: the General Household Survey, the Health Survey for England and the ONS Omnibus Survey. Findings suggest that around a fifth of men and just under a tenth of women can be defined as 'binge' drinkers using this measure. Another unit-based definition found in research literature is the consumption of half the recommended weekly intake in a single session[4] (for example Webb *et al.*, 1996).

Unit-based definitions have been criticised as they ignore a number of factors that can influence the way in which a given amount of alcohol affects an individual. These may include body weight, alcohol tolerance, the swiftness with which drinks are consumed, and the amount of food an individual has in their system. Midanik (1999) found a considerable variation between those who regularly 'binged' according to a unit-based definition and those who reported regularly feeling drunk. The study found that the subjective measure was a better predictor of various social and health outcomes.

---

3   *Sensible Drinking: The Report of an Inter-Departmental Working Group*, Department of Health, December 1995.
4   This works out as 11 or more units for men and 7 or more for women.

The approach taken for the current study relies on a subjective definition of binge drinking. The young people who participated in the research reported feeling drunk either on a weekly basis, or at least once a month - a definition that relied on young people's individual perceptions of what 'being drunk' involves. (Further details on how young people were selected for the study are provided later in this chapter).

Binge drinking and young people

Research suggests that young adults aged between 18 and 24 are more likely than other adults to binge drink (Moore *et al.*, 1994) and that binge drinking is the most common form of hazardous alcohol consumption among young people (Murgraff *et al.*, 1999). Furthermore, there is concern that both binge drinking and overall alcohol consumption are on the rise among young people in the U.K. (Harnett *et al.*, 2000; Webb *et al.*, 1996).

Other groups who are more likely to binge drink include young males, manual workers, single people and those who do most of their drinking at the weekend (Moore *et al.*, 1994). Aitken's (1985) observations of young adult drinkers in licensed premises found that drinking appeared to be heavier in groups. All-male groups drank most heavily, while all-female groups appeared to drink more heavily than the females in mixed company. Both Moore and Aitken found that binge drinking was associated with drinking lager.

As Rehm *et al.* (1996) point out, drinking is a social act and different drinking patterns are associated with different social interactions. The social situations and behaviours that surround binge drinking play a crucial part in determining its outcomes. It therefore becomes necessary to investigate the social context within which people binge drink, in order to understand both drinking patterns and their consequences. For this study, which focuses on young adults, it is necessary to understand the particular age-related social and cultural factors that affect their drinking behaviour during this stage of their lives, as well as the influences on alcohol consumption that operate in society as a whole.

Alcohol, crime and disorder

The association between alcohol and crime and disorder is well documented in research literature. However the relationship is far from straightforward, and the precise nature of the links is the subject of continuing debate.

As Deehan (1999) points out in her review of the research literature, alcohol is most frequently linked to crimes of an aggressive or violent nature. According to the British Crime Survey (BCS), a third of violent incidents between strangers and a fifth of violent incidents between acquaintances take place in or around a pub or club. In half of the stranger incidents and a third of those between acquaintances, the victim felt their attacker had been 'under the influence' of alcohol (Mattinson, 2001). Alcohol also features prominently in instances of harassment. Seventeen per cent of BCS respondents who had been insulted, pestered or intimidated thought this had happened because the offender was drunk. Drunkenness was one of the three reasons most commonly given by victims for this type of offence being committed (Budd and Sims, 2001).

However, the relationship between alcohol and aggression is far from being a direct causal one. Researchers have pointed out the role of situation and expectations in incidents of alcohol-related violence (Brown *et al.*, 1980; Graham *et al.*, 1998), as well as factors relating to the cultural and institutional context of licensed premises as opposed to other drinking settings (Homel *et al.*, 2001). What is clear is that certain forms of criminal and disorderly behaviour often occur within the night-time economy. Marsh and Kibby (1992) found that violence and disorder in the night-time economy is concentrated on weekend nights, with around half the incidents in public houses occurring between 11 pm and midnight on a Friday or Saturday. To reflect the key role played by the social setting in alcohol-related crime and disorder, the current study selected young people who regularly drank in licensed premises.

Binge drinking, young people and crime

As Deehan (1999) points out, alcohol-related crimes are associated mainly with the young, particularly young males whose offence involves aggression. The evidence suggests that there are factors besides alcohol consumption which have an impact on involvement in crime and disorder among this age group. For example, the British Crime Survey indicates that 16- to 24-year-olds are the most likely age group to commit violent offences against a stranger, but are no more likely to be judged as 'under the influence' than perpetrators aged 25 and over (Mattinson, 2001).

Although there are many studies that examine the links between alcohol and crime and disorder, relatively few have looked specifically at the relationship between binge drinking and crime. However Deehan *et al.*'s (2002) investigation of people arrested late at night in city centre areas found that the majority of arrestees were drunk, and that almost half of intoxicated arrestees were aged between 18 and 24.

Cookson (1992) surveyed convicted male offenders aged between 17 and 21, and found a significant association between drinking at the time of the offence and violent offences. Violent offenders who had been drinking were more likely than other groups who had been drinking to have consumed significantly more alcohol than was usual for them, although they were no more likely to claim that they had been drunk at the time of the offence.

Evidence suggests that binge drinking may be linked to an increased risk of injury arising from an assault. Shepherd and Brickley (1996) studied males aged between 18 and 35 who attended a large Accident and Emergency Department following an assault. They found that consumption of more than ten units of alcohol in the six hours prior to the assault was associated with injury. Injury cases consumed more alcohol and were more likely to binge drink than the control group, who could not be differentiated from the case group on most demographic indicators.

Midanik (1999) found that subjective measures of frequency of drunkenness helped to explain variations in adverse social consequences for participants in the 1995 US National Alcohol Survey. These consequences included arguments, fights, police warnings, arrests and accidents. Although the models produced were only moderately effective, it is interesting to note that subjective measures of drunkenness were a better predictor of outcomes than a more objective measure based on the number of drinks consumed per session.

As stated earlier, social context is an important factor in understanding both drinking patterns and outcomes (Rehm *et al.*, 1996). Studies have shown that the drinking environment can have a key influence – Homel *et al.*, (2001) found that violent incidents are exacerbated by noisiness, crowding, poorly maintained or unclean premises, inadequate seating and door policy, and irresponsible serving practices. The influence of the drinking environment is explored in this research.

Binge drinking and risk-taking

As well as crime and disorder, research has linked binge drinking to other forms of risky or hazardous behaviour, such as unsafe sex. Evidence suggests that excessive drinking before sex is strongly associated with unprotected sex, although it may be the case that "a third variable such as arousal-seeking mediates between these two risky behaviours" (Murgraff *et al.*, 1999). The desire for excitement may also play a part in other risk-taking behaviours associated with drinking alcohol, such as those that lead to disorderly or criminal behaviour. The current study explores a range of risk-taking behaviours associated with drinking alcohol, including sexual risks, and examines the links between different types of risk behaviour, the effects of alcohol, and broader attitudinal factors.

Until recently there has been relatively little research examining the relationship between binge drinking and illegal drug use, although Measham (1996) found a link between heavier use of illicit drugs and heavier use of alcohol. For a long time it was thought that alcohol and illicit drugs did not tend to co-exist, and even that illicit drug use led to a reduction in drinking consumption (see review by Newburn and Shiner, 2001); studies such as Measham's reflect a growing awareness in recent years that the two may be more closely related than this. Several young people in the current study reported illegal drug use; the links between patterns of drug use and alcohol consumption were explored in the research.

This study

The current study was designed to explore the social context of alcohol consumption among young adults who regularly binge drink. The research focused on young people aged between 18 and 24 (the age group found in previous research to be most likely to engage in binge drinking).

A qualitative methodology was chosen as the most suitable approach for an in-depth exploration of the social context that surrounds binge drinking and associated behaviours. As Rehm et al., (1996) argue, drinking alcohol is primarily a social act, making it necessary to investigate the social context of binge drinking in order to understand patterns and outcomes. Qualitative approaches are therefore appropriate because of their emphasis on "context-embedded behaviour" (Gilbert, 1990).

Previous studies of the links between binge drinking and disorder have been concentrated on quite specific samples (e.g. students, arrestees, patients in Accident and Emergency Departments). One aim of the current study was to explore the links between binge drinking and disorder among the wider population of young adult binge drinkers. It should be stressed, however, that the qualitative nature of this research means that it cannot be held to be representative of the population of young adult binge drinkers in England and Wales as a whole.

The research consisted of 16 focus group discussions with young people, carried out in 8 locations (2 groups per location). The size of the focus groups ranged between 5 and 11 young people, with 123 young people participating in total. To target young people with direct experience of a busy weekend night-time economy, the locations chosen were a mixture of market towns, large towns, cities and metropolitan areas.

All young people recruited drank in a pub, bar or club at least once a month. Subjective perceptions of frequency of drunkenness were chosen as the defining criteria of 'binge drinkers'. Groups were divided into those who reported feeling drunk at least once a week, and those who felt drunk less than once a week but at least once a month. Ten groups were of young people who had been involved in offending or disorder after drinking during the previous year, as either perpetrator, victim or both. The young binge drinkers in the remaining 6 groups did not appear to fit into the categories defined as 'offender' or 'victim'; however, the majority had behaved in ways that put them 'at risk' after drinking.

Genders, age and occupational status were also taken into account in the composition of the groups (see Appendix A for further details).

A note on interpretation

When interpreting findings from qualitative research, it should be remembered that results are not based on quantitative statistical evidence but on a small sample of a cross-section of young people. To aid the anonymity of our respondents when quoted, each verbatim comment is identified by a person's gender, age and occupational status.

Young people were recruited according to three categories of behaviour and experience while drinking: those who had behaved in a disorderly way, victims of crime or disorder, and those who have put themselves at risk, consciously or otherwise. However, it soon became clear that the distinctions were not exclusive, and that a group of 'victims' may actually talk more freely about their disorderly or offending behaviour. Therefore, we have not identified verbatim comments according to whether the participant was involved in an 'offender', 'victim', or 'at risk' group discussion, as this may be misleading to the reader.

Quotes from individuals have been chosen to illustrate the range of viewpoints on each key theme in the research. Only a small minority of the quotes selected incorporate an exchange of views between two people in the group; these quotes are indicated by a plural attribute. This does not mean that discussion and debate within the focus groups did not occur; indeed, in many of the groups the discussion was very animated. Issues which generated more lively debate are highlighted in the main body of the report; in general, when opposing viewpoints are put across for any particular point, this should be taken as indicating that the issue was a subject of disagreement and discussion within at least some of the groups. A more detailed account of how the focus groups were analysed and interpreted is provided in Appendix A.

2   Binge drinking behaviour

A key objective of the research was to gain a sense of the overall drinking patterns among the 18- to 24-year-old age group, and to understand the role that 'binge' drinking plays within their lives. The section explores:

- the typical 'big night out': how often it happens, what is drunk, and whether drinking binges are planned or spontaneous;
- positive and negative images of getting drunk; in particular, perceptions of 'letting yourself go' versus perceptions of 'being out of control';
- the motivations behind getting drunk, and getting uncontrollably drunk or binge drinking; and
- the role of illegal drugs while drinking alcohol, and usage of and attitudes towards alcohol compared with other drugs.

Choice and control: getting drunk

One of the criteria for recruiting the focus groups was the frequency with which the young people got drunk. Groups were divided into those who got drunk at least once a week and those who got drunk less often than once a week but at least once a month, with 'mixed frequency' groups in some areas. This was done to compare young people's attitudes to drinking and behaviour on a night out according to the frequency with which they got drunk.

Those who got drunk less frequently tended to have a 'big night out' every two or three weeks. This was usually on a Friday or Saturday, although non-worker and student groups were more likely to also have heavy drinking sessions on other days of the week. Among drinkers who had a big night at least once a week, some confined their activities to a Friday or Saturday night while others had mid-week drinking sessions in addition to this. Students and manual workers were more likely to have drinking sessions mid-week as well as at the end of the week.

Despite these differences, drinking patterns *during* the 'big nights out' in question were remarkably similar across all groups. Although the amount drunk and the drinks of choice varied according to individuals' taste and tolerance, all the young people drew a distinction between the nights when they go out and have a 'social' drink and the nights when they expect to get drunk. On the 'big nights', they described drinking with the deliberate *intention* of getting drunk.

Many mixed different kinds of drink in order to enhance or accelerate this process; others drank at home before they went out or deliberately drank quickly. Several were aware that particular types of drink have a stronger effect on them, and chose those drinks for that reason.

> I can't drink wine because it goes straight to my head, but if I am going out to get pissed and I don't go out until 8.30pm, I think, "I will have a couple of glasses of wine before I go out, so I am halfway there"   (Female, 18-20, manual worker)

> Me and my friend have a rule that if we go out, eating is cheating. If you eat it is going to soak up the alcohol   (Female, 18-20, non-manual worker)

These statements suggest that the 'big night out', along with the heavy drinking and drunkenness that accompany it, is usually anticipated in advance. This is not always the case, however. While most plan ahead to an extent, others say that the wilder evenings are often the unexpected ones. For these, spontaneity can be the key to a good night out.

> When you go out for just a couple and you end up staying out all night and getting nailed, they are the best nights   (Male, 20-24, manual worker)

Although the young people frequently anticipated getting drunk, most reported occasions when they ended up getting *more* drunk than they actually wanted to. One reason the young people gave for getting 'too drunk' was that a person's perceived tolerance to alcohol can vary from night to night, making it hard to predict the effects that a certain amount of drink will have. Another was that the line between a person perceiving themselves as slightly drunk or very drunk can be crossed very easily; just one drink may be enough to move a young person from feeling 'tipsy' to feeling 'hammered'. The young people used arguments like these to explain why it was hard for them to 'pace themselves', limit the amount that they drink on a night out, or judge the point at which 'very drunk' may become 'too drunk'. These perceptions were also a factor in the nights where a 'social drink' developed into an unplanned drinking session or 'binge'.

> It varies every time you drink, because sometimes you go out and drink ten pints and then other times you can go out and drink four or five and be really pissed and not know what you are doing   (Male, 21-24, manual worker)

> You will be drinking and feel like you are getting there and you will have another one and feel slaughtered or completely gone, and you will have another one and you will either be on the floor or dancing like a lunatic, falling all over the place   (Male, 18-21, student)

This lack of control may be related to a lack of experience, particularly among the younger people interviewed. While all the young people enjoyed getting drunk, most felt some degree of caution about getting *very* drunk. Some worried about behaving inappropriately or did not like the idea that they might forget what had happened to them the next day. Others simply did not want to spoil their nights out by making themselves ill.

> *People come up to you the next day and say, "I can't believe what you were doing last night", and things like that. You don't want to be embarrassed by yourself*
> (Female, 21-24, student)

This desire to remain *relatively* sober, however, was not always kept once the young people were in the drinking environment. While a few were able to recognise when they were getting drunk and slow their pace, others could not recognise how drunk they were, or found they lost their reservations once they became drunk and carried on regardless.

> *After midnight I have had a few, and I am getting really tipsy, and I will just stop*
> (Female, 21-24, student)

> *If you go out on a night you just carry on, no matter how drunk you seem to get*
> (Female, 18-20, manual worker)

For some of the young people, getting *too* drunk was simply not a concern. A few argued that they reached a point while drinking after which any extra drinks made no difference to their mental or physical state, a process described by some as 'drinking yourself sober'. Worryingly, young people who made these claims felt that they were ultimately 'in control' of themselves and the situation, despite the large amounts of alcohol they had in their system.

> *Once I get to a certain point my body thinks I am drinking water or something and just goes normal*
> (Female, 18-20, non-worker)

Meanwhile, a significant minority was happy to admit to losing control. These people regarded events such as illness or memory loss as an accepted part of the night's fun, and found it amusing to 'piece the evening together' with their friends afterwards. In some cases, it took quite extreme incidents such as being hospitalised with alcohol poisoning to make young people start thinking about moderating their drinking.

> *That is the best thing about it, you can't remember half of what you have done. You have to rely on your mates to tell you what you have done the night before*
> (Male, 18-20, manual worker)

If I am drunk and sick then I know I have enjoyed myself (Female, 18-20, non-worker)

We all went up town, I was knocking these shots back and I don't remember anything... It was just like stomach pumps and all that black stuff they throw down you, and that was the only time it slowed me down (Female, 21-24, non-worker)

Both men and women reported drinking with the intention of getting drunk, and both men and women described drinking fast, mixing their drinks and losing control while drunk. However, some young people perceived a difference between male and female drinkers. Both young men and young women described women as less single-minded in their drinking; less likely to goad each other into drinking too much, too quickly, and more likely to take a break from drinking in order to dance or talk. Some also made the point that it is easier for young women to switch to water or soft drinks without 'losing face' among their peers.

Lads go out to get drunk, lasses go out to have a good time
(Female, 20-25, non-manual worker)

I find it very awkward to go up to the bar and say, "Can I have an orange juice?"

I think it's harder for boys because it's the ego, a male thing, you don't want to act dainty with other males (Males, 18-20, students)

However, is should be recognised that gender distinctions were not drawn in all groups, and that some of the more indulgent women and more cautious men may have disagreed with these descriptions. Some young women admitted to the same drinking patterns and behaviour as their male counterparts.

I reckon people have always been drunk... It is just girls are doing it now as well

Lad-ette culture (Females, 21-24, students)

Escaping the everyday: motivations for drinking

The young people described getting drunk as good fun, or a 'laugh'. It is a social activity that they are happy to join in with; something that they do with friends, to relax and to enjoy themselves. Having fun is the ultimate aim of the night out, but within this there are a variety of different motivations which can play a part in encouraging binge drinking.

Sometimes it is purely to have a laugh (Female, 21-24, student)

One motivation the young people identified was a desire for the social confidence that comes with 'Dutch courage'. For example, young people may find that they are less shy about talking to someone they do not know very well, or dancing in front of other people in a night-club, if they have had something to drink. The desire for confidence emerged particularly strongly as an immediate motivation in two of the female groups, and appears to relate to concerns about self-image and appearance. However, both men and women mentioned an increase in self-confidence as one of the positive effects of drinking, particularly where this helped them improve their communications with the opposite sex. A few said that drinking allowed them to relax and 'be themselves', which suggests that they may feel they lack the confidence to 'be themselves' in everyday life.

You don't care what anyone thinks. If you are sober you might just sit in the corner, not look at anyone (Female, 18-20, manual worker)

I am dead skinny when I am drunk, I would wear the skimpiest little bikini and I would look fab in it (Female, 21-24, non-worker)

With my mate, like, if we were clubbing or at a party he wouldn't dance or speak to girls or anything unless he had a drink (Female, 18-20, non-worker)

Another motivation is to relieve stress. This was particularly likely to be mentioned by those who work full-time, especially those who said that they did not enjoy their job. Friday night is seen as the time to 'let yourself go' and forget the frustrations of the working week. A few say this adds to the intensity of the weekend's activities and means they drink more than they would do otherwise – the urge is to let off as much steam as possible between Friday and Monday. Young workers are more likely than older ones to be in a junior position and to do relatively menial work, which means that frustration at work may be a key motivation for this group.

I would say eight out of ten people in [town name] don't like their job, and the weekends are like, heaven-sent... Friday night you almost panic, you feel like you want the best time you think you can have and it's every single time

(Male, 21-24, manual worker)

After a week of pretty unpleasant, tedious, boring work you are going to want to have a blow out at the weekend (Male, 21-24, non-manual worker)

Young people who were unemployed were also motivated by the idea of forgetting their day-to-day worries; however, they were less likely to use the term 'stress' and more likely to say that drinking helps them to 'take their mind off things'. The focus on stress and problems was less strong among the student groups, although a few mentioned stress in relation to exams. They too were motivated by the escape from the everyday, but are more likely to emphasise the 'laugh' of getting drunk than to describe it as a release or relief.

A lot on your mind... Trying to block things out (Female, non-worker, 18-20)

It's alright, it takes your mind off your problems (Male, 21-24, non-worker)

When you are drinking you just have a laugh and do what you want, it makes a change from doing whatever you do in the day, whether it is working or studying

(Male, 18-21, student)

Many of the young people identified the 'escapism' that motivates their binge drinking. The urge to get drunk is strong, but so too is the urge to get out of the house and do something different. A few argued that they would not necessarily go out drinking so much if there were other options.

You become a different person, well, not become a different person, but you can kind of escape the reality of what you do in the week and that (Female, 18-20, manual worker)

But what is the alternative... Where can you go at 11pm? ... If you didn't want to drink you would just be sitting at home watching television all the time and that's not healthy (Male, 21-24, non-manual worker)

For those whose circumstances were especially stressful or constraining, such as single mothers, drinking was particularly likely to be associated with personal freedom, self-indulgence and escape from day-to-day pressures.

*It just takes away your problems… You can just laugh and see things rosy and, you
know, I have got until next morning* (Female, 21-24, non-worker)

Enhancing the evening: binge drinking and illegal drug use

The role of illegal drugs in a 'big night out' varies a great deal from person to person.
While the majority of the people interviewed talked only about their drinking habits, there
were several cannabis smokers, and some who use harder drugs.

Most cannabis smokers said that cannabis did not play a major role in their binge drinking
sessions. It was more likely to be used at the end of a big night out, when the young person
was relaxing back at home. Some expressed caution about mixing alcohol and cannabis
because they were worried about the combination making them feel sick; however, they did
not seem to perceive mixing alcohol and cannabis as actually being dangerous.

*Most of the time when you come home you have a couple of spliffs to wind down
from the night, and then get your head down. You can't really smoke a spliff in some
clubs, because you get a raid. Sometimes you can and people take the odd spliff
with them* (Male, 18-20, manual worker)

I don't mix the two together because it can make you ill (Male, 18-21, student)

For users of harder drugs such as speed, ecstasy and cocaine, these drugs played a part in
some 'big nights out', although this depended on where people were going and who they
were going with. For some, taking these drugs was part of the plan for an evening in which
alcohol had no place. Their focus was on the music and dancing in a particular night-club,
and mixing the drugs with drink was viewed as pointless or dangerous.

I do go to clubs now and then where I will have one [Ecstasy tablet] *and I fully enjoy
my night, but I don't mix them, I never would* (Male, 20-24, manual worker)

A few were more blasé about hard drugs, and were happier to use them in a variety of
settings and perhaps on impulse. Although not all of these young people used hard drugs
regularly, they did give the impression of using hard drugs more frequently than the young
people who only used them in night-clubs. They were more relaxed about the risks of mixing
these drugs with alcohol, and some said that doing this has what they regard as
advantages. They argued that using hard drugs enables them to drink more, or perks them
up when they have drunk too much and allows them to see the night through to the end.

When you've had a few to drink you start to feel a bit drowsy, and you do it [Ecstasy] and it just brings you right up again (Male, 21-24, manual worker)

You can drink more when you have coke and pills and that (Male, 18-20, manual worker)

Mixing drink and drugs was seen by some as desirable in order to prolong, or intensify, the high. This view appears to be a similar, but more extreme, version of the mindset that encourages other young people to keep on drinking, drink quickly or mix their drinks.

You just want more stimulants in your system, get as wrecked as possible (Female, 18-20, student)

If you are going out to get drunk, anything that releases any chemical in your brain, you are going to get as much of it as you can (Male, 21-24, non-manual worker)

Conclusions

While this chapter provides an overview of binge drinking behaviour among young adults, certain factors are particularly relevant when considering the relationship between alcohol and disorder in the night-time economy.

The extent to which binge drinking sessions are or are not anticipated has implications for our understanding of young people's behaviour on a night out. The findings show that young people often go out with the definite intention of getting drunk, and that many deliberately accelerate or intensify their drunkenness by mixing drinks, drinking before they go out, or drinking beverages that they know have a strong effect on them. On the other hand, young people also describe getting drunk when they do not intend to do so; it seems likely that lack of experience plays a part in this. This suggests that there are two distinct but related characteristics of this age group that inform their binge drinking behaviour: a desire to push their limits in terms of how drunk they get, and an inability to judge these limits. The fact that young people find it difficult to predict how a given quantity of drink will affect them may support the argument of Midanik (1999), who suggests that subjective definitions of drunkenness may be more effective than objective measures of consumption when exploring the outcomes of binge drinking.

While many young people were keen to get *very* drunk on a night out, most expressed a degree of caution about getting *too* drunk. However, there were a significant minority who saw illness, memory loss and loss of control as part of the fun of a night out, as well as a few who claimed that they never lose control no matter how much they drink. Furthermore, the desire to push the limits and difficulty judging the limits common to most of the young people meant that even those who were more cautious in theory were not always cautious in practice. Men were commonly described as less likely to regulate their drinking than women, although there was some debate about this issue. Certainly a number of UK studies have suggested that binge drinking is more common among young men than young women (Aitken, 1985; Moore *et al.*, 1994; Webb *et al.*, 1996).

The most common reason given for binge drinking is enjoyment. This supports the findings of Webb *et al.*, (1996), who found that the overwhelming majority of both male and female university students said that they drank alcohol for 'pleasure'. Within the broader agenda of 'having fun', young people described getting drunk in order to relieve stress, forget their everyday worries and feel more confident socially. These factors also feature in Webb et al's research: 'increased confidence' is particularly prominent, given by a fifth of men and a third of women as a reason for drinking. Young people in the current study associated drinking with personal freedom, self-indulgence and an escape from daily routines – factors which seem likely to encourage more extreme drinking behaviour.

Users of illegal drugs appeared to be split into those who preferred to keep their drink and drug use separate, and those who were happier to contemplate mixing. Those who mixed alcohol with drugs such as speed, ecstasy or cocaine argued that it allowed them to prolong the night out and keep drinking for longer than usual. This recalls the findings of Measham (1996), who found that heavier use of illicit drugs is linked with heavier use of alcohol. This attitude appears as an extreme version of the escapist mindset and desire to push the limits that were common to the majority of the young people.

The attitudes and motivations surrounding binge drinking can affect not only what is drunk, how much and when, but also the young people's behaviour while out drinking. For example, Aitken's (1985) observational research found that groups of heavy drinkers were more "noisy and boisterous" than other groups of drinkers, even at the start of the evening before much alcohol had been consumed. The influence of these key factors on young people's experience of crime and disorder on a night out is explored in subsequent chapters.

3   In it together? The social context of binge drinking

This research aims to explore the 'social context' of binge drinking. The overall social context can be seen as consisting of several aspects, including peer group norms and behaviour, broader cultural norms and the environment in which 'binge drinking' takes place.

These features of the social context influence the drinking patterns and attitudes towards drinking discussed in the previous section. Furthermore, these factors can have an impact on young drinkers' involvement in crime, disorder and risk taking.

Fun with friends: the peer group influence

Drinking is seen as integral to a night out. As well as stemming from wider aspects of British culture, this attitude seems to have been at least partly created within the young people's friendship groups. Binge drinking is described as a shared activity, and is used by some young people to help establish and maintain friendships. For most it is the 'group' aspect of the drinking session that makes getting drunk so much fun.

> It is more like a social thing, as long as everyone with you is laughing, then you just want to laugh with them   (Female, 21-24, student)

According to some young people, friends were likely to discourage them if they attempted to stick to soft drinks. This was not recognised as 'peer pressure', as the young people were usually quite happy to be 'persuaded' to drink something alcoholic instead. For many, the fact that everybody around them on a night out drinks alcohol meant that soft drinks were simply not an option which they had, or would, consider. As we have seen, a key motivation for drinking among this age group relates to confidence; it seems likely that young adults may be less confident than older people to break away from peer group norms.

> When you get to the pub, no matter how good your intentions might be to have an orange and lemonade your friends say, "Oh no, have a pint" and it is so much easier to stick to that drink   (Male, 21-24, non-manual worker)

You are pushed into it because you enjoy it (Female, 18-20, non-worker)

When my friends are really pissed and I am not I really hate it
(Female, 21-24, non-manual worker)

Several young people said that their behaviour on a night out varies depending on the particular group of friends they are with. Some tend to drink more if they were with friends who also drink heavily. Others have different friendship groups that drink a similar amount, but behave differently when they are drunk: some sit down and talk, some dance, some take drugs, and so on.

When you are with one group of friends you might act completely different to when you are with another... One group of mates I go out with get leathered and sit in the corner and just chat all night, and another just go mad (Female, 20-24, manual worker)

I got into a bad crowd and every weekend we would be out as if it was going out of fashion. And it was a case of, it didn't matter what it was, if you could get your hands on it you would take it [a drug] (Female, 21-24, non-worker)

As with the drinking itself, it is the shared nature of drunken activities that helps to create the enjoyment. This means that young people's behaviour on a night out is influenced by more than just the alcohol and their personal preferences. For some, the gender mix within the group was key. A 'girls' night out' or 'boys' night out' could be viewed as very different from a mixed gathering, although opinions varied among both men and women as to whether the presence of the opposite sex encouraged or discouraged more extreme behaviour.

I reckon I get more drunk when I go out with the girls... Because you just think, I am going to be really silly tonight and go mad

A lot of my male friends, they will encourage me to drink. Like we will have races and stuff, and we will drink shots (Females, 18-20, manual workers)

It's more of a competition with the boys. Trying to keep up with the blokes

I tend to show off in front of girls and not boys. You're just trying to impress
(Males, 18-20, students)

Some of the men interviewed, particularly at the younger end of the spectrum, said that they are 'encouraged' quite forcefully to drink by their male friends. This suggests that younger men tend to be less secure in their self-image, and perhaps feel the need to prove themselves as 'one of the lads' more keenly. Once again, it seems likely that this relates to the relative lack of confidence among younger age groups when it comes to standing out from the crowd.

> *Usually everyone is drinking around you and you are under a lot of pressure to keep going*　　　　　　　　　　　　　　　　　　　　(Male, 18-20, manual worker)

> *They're egging you on, like, "Aaargh, go on"*　　　　　　　(Male, 18-20, student)

As we shall see, friendship groups and the norms under which they operate can have a key influence on whether or not a night on the town ends in trouble. The sense that everyone is 'in it together' can influence young people's perceptions of disorder or risk-taking on a night out by making them feel safer, and in some cases may lessen the sense of responsibility that they have for the things they do while drunk. In addition, the presence of friends can reassure people that they will be looked after by others should they become too drunk to take care of themselves. In this way, companions on a night out affect overall attitudes and behaviour as well as drinking patterns.

The importance of identity: wider social groups

As 'young adults', 18- to 24-year-olds are often still in the process of defining their identity as adults, discovering who they are, what they like and where their limits lie. This is likely to be part of the reason why the peer group influence is so strong for some, particularly those in their late teens. While the desire to socialise and bond with others can influence behaviour at any age, young adults are more likely to be at a stage where identifying themselves with a group of friends seems crucial for confidence and social success.

> *Just to fit in, I suppose, with my friends. I am not so different from them but we are doing different things at different levels… Drinking and getting tipsy is like, "Whoa, here she comes"*　　　　　　　　　　　　　　　　　　(Female, 21-24, student)

> *You go into work and talk about the night out and the night before. You get quite a good buzz when you are talking to all your mates*　　　(Male, 18-20, manual worker)

As well as influencing behaviour within the friendship group, this sometimes affects the way in which different groups of young drinkers relate to each other. The fact that the night-time economy throws groups of young people with different affiliations together can mean that it is the arena in which broader social tensions are played out, as when there are 'student' pubs and pubs for 'locals' in a particular area.

People can get beaten up for the way they look. People can see if you're a student and it's "Knock him up, student wanker", I've heard that, "Oh, he's got spiky hair, get him"

I come from [area name]. It isn't the nicest place in the world, it's a totally different world, and when these people come into town they feel alienated as well and want to establish their turf
(Males, 18-21, students)

This is sometimes compounded by the fact that young people are more likely to identify themselves strongly with particular fashion or music styles, which may also dictate the particular bars, pubs and night-clubs where different groups feel comfortable going. Clothes and locations were seen as carrying a particular 'badge of allegiance' by some of the groups, who described a tendency for both staff and clientele to judge on appearance when they are trying to identify potential troublemakers.

If you have got long hair like me and are big on black clothes and stuff, you just don't go into places where everybody is looking for a fight
(Male, 18-20, non-manual worker)

They go on appearance, a lot of them. If you've got lots of big rings sometimes they don't let you into the club, they tell you you've got to take all of that jewellery off
(Male, 21-24, manual worker)

This emphasis on 'social identity' is another aspect of the social context that may relate to a lack of confidence among this age group. Young people who identify themselves strongly with a group or trend may be unsure of their own identity and looking for ways to assert it, while feeling threatened by individuals from different social groups could also stem from lack of confidence.

Who drinks where: the impact of environment

Although preferences and experiences differed, the groups generally agreed that the particular drinking venue can have an impact on what they drink and how much. This point was also mentioned frequently in relation to drug-taking. Both those who took drugs and those who did not described particular environments where drug-taking is more common, more accepted, or feels more 'natural'.

> *If you are in a pub you will have a beer or whatever, but if you are in a club you will probably get a bottle*   (Male, 20-24, manual worker)

> *I think the whole drugs thing happens more with the big night-clubs, drum and bass clubs, everybody's on something in them*   (Male, 21-24, manual worker)

The young people frequently named particular venues or parts of town that were perceived as 'trouble spots'; places where fights were more likely, that were best avoided on a night out. Sometimes these comments were made in relation to the reputations of particular pubs or clubs. In other cases, these perceptions related to the judgements that young people made about other young drinkers, based on their appearance or social group.

> [Town name] *has got a really big jungle based theme, I haven't been involved myself but I have watched so many fights*   (Male, 21-24, manual worker)

> *I find it hard to go out in* [the City Centre] *at the weekends. It's very towny, very aggressive*

> *Especially on a Friday night, you get all the scallies that have just been paid*
> (Female and male, 18-21, students)

Some young people perceived their drinking environment as more threatening than others, and thought that fights would be more likely. This finding was often related to the broader social tensions and problems that existed in certain areas. Factors that were mentioned by the young people included:

- antagonism between students and locals;
- antagonism between conventional and traveller communities;
- racial tensions; and
- people living in 'rough'/deprived areas, where fighting, carrying weapons and other forms of offending or violence were seen as commonplace.

More broadly, features of the town centre environment clearly influenced what happened to the young people on a night out. Where bars, night-clubs and streets were crowded, this was seen by some as adding to the tensions that made 'trouble' on more likely. Furthermore, the array of available pubs, bars and night-clubs in a small space and the common pattern of going on a 'crawl' on a big night out added to the 'unplanned' aspect of many of the young people's binge drinking sessions.

> *You know where you are going to start, you just don't know where you are going to finish up. You start off somewhere, and then you just move on*   (Male, 18-20, manual worker)

> *You'll have nights where you end up somewhere you didn't expect*
> (Male, 18-21, student)

Cultural context: the nation's youth

Both the thriving night-time economy, and the way in which social group norms encourage binge drinking, could be viewed aspects of a wider 'drinking culture' in England and Wales. A few young people clearly identified binge drinking as part of 'British culture'; others said that it was the norm among their family or community as well as their peer group. For some young people, drinking and getting drunk were so much a part of the established social routine that it was difficult for them to think about their motivations for it.

> *We are a culture that goes out and gets drunk, and we don't go out to drink, we go out to get drunk*   (Female, 21-24, non-manual worker)

> *You don't have to know the reason for it. You just do it anyway. Everybody does it, it is the way the world is*   (Male, 18-20, non-manual worker)

Alongside attitudes towards drinking that are common among the general population, age and life-stage were cited as influences on young people's drinking habits. While some young people felt that their behaviour might not change much as they got older, others had already modified their drinking in response to work or family responsibilities.

> *I can't go out much since I had the baby. I have calmed down a lot*

> *If you have got commitments it is not the same*   (Males, 18-20, manual workers)

Some felt that they were at a stage in their lives where they could put having a good time above other considerations – where they could push the limits of how much they drink or how much money they spend on a night out, without having to worry about the long-term consequences. Here we may be seeing evidence of a 'youth culture', that shapes attitudes to drinking alongside the broader national culture.

> It changes the day when you are working, I don't think you tend to get hammered in the week then. You can't get hammered and go out to work   (Male, 18-20, student)

> I have got more money [when I'm working], I can spend more on drink then. Every single night   (Male, 18-20, manual worker)

Conclusions

While the 'social context' of binge drinking among young adults is informed by a number of elements, certain factors are particularly relevant when considering the relationship between alcohol and disorder in the night-time economy.

One is that binge drinking is often so routine that young people find it difficult to explain why they do it. As this chapter demonstrates, the acceptability of binge drinking is established both within the young people's immediate friendship group and through their perceptions of wider cultural norms. This can affect young people's ability to regulate their drinking, even when they begin an evening with cautious intentions, and has implications for policies that aim to reduce alcohol consumption among young adults. Webb et al., (1996) found that a third of male students and a fifth of female students reported 'habit' as a reason for drinking.

The desire to fit in with friends is a key influence on both drinking patterns and behaviour while drunk. Many of the young people described behaving differently on nights out with different groups of friends. Young people usually attributed this to their personal desire to join in the fun, although some – particularly young males drinking in all-male groups – described more overt forms of peer pressure. Some of the descriptions of drinking among same-sex groups recall Aitken's (1985) finding that people in single-sex groups tended to drink more heavily: however, different individuals in a discussion often had different views on this issue. Young people's accounts certainly seem to support Aitken's observations of the overall impact that drinking companions have on drinking patterns. His study found that the average amount consumed by drinking companions accounted for 62 per cent of the variation in alcohol consumption by men, and 42 per cent of the variation in women.

In terms of the broader social context of the town or city, the night-time economy may be the arena where tensions and antagonisms between different social groups are played out. Different groups, such as students and locals in a university town, are often identified with different music styles, fashion styles or drinking venues. These factors can have an influence on the areas of a town or city that are perceived as threatening or non-threatening by different types of young people on a night out, and may serve to aggravate confrontation where there is hostility between groups. Many young people identified particular pubs, clubs or parts of town as 'trouble spots' on a night out. The reputation of individual venues and areas often seemed to be related to young people's social *judgements* about the clientele. Research has highlighted the role of *expectations* of a situation in fuelling aggression among drinkers (Brown *et al.*, 1980; Graham *et al.*, 1998; Turning Point, 1998); these factors may be relevant here.

A key observation is that many of the factors discussed relate particularly strongly to young adults, rather than being more general features of the night-time economy and British attitudes towards drinking. Specifically, their relative lack of both confidence and responsibility when compared with older age groups features prominently in their experience of binge drinking. This suggests that policies which aim to tackle alcohol-related disorder should take account of factors relating to age and life-stage.

The social context of binge drinking is also the social context of disorder in the night-time economy. The influence of this context on young people's experience of crime and disorder is explored in subsequent chapters.

4   Being in a bubble – the effects of binge drinking

The research aims to explore the *consequences* of binge drinking. The consequences that are ultimately of interest for this study are those that relate to offending, anti-social behaviour and risk-taking on a night out. However, the more immediate consequences of binge drinking are the effects that it can have on young people's attitudes, mood and interaction with others. To understand *why* some young people get involved in crime and disorder when they have been drinking, it is necessary to understand the overall impact that alcohol has on their feelings and behaviour.

Confidence and consequences

As we have seen, the young people enjoy getting drunk because it is fun, and seek the confidence boost and escape from the normal routine that getting drunk brings as part of the fun. They described losing their inhibitions, finding it easier to talk to people and approach strangers. They worry less about what they look like, and are more adventurous in what they do. They are also more easily amused, both by themselves and by the things and people around them, and are likely to feel more positive towards the world in general.

> *You talk crap, you dance crap, but you don't care about it, you don't look at yourself and think, "I am dancing really naff here", you're quite happy to jump on a table or do something stupid*
>   (Male, 18-21, student)

> *You feel you can do anything when you are drunk. Nearly anything*

> *You think you are six foot tall and ten foot wide*
>   (Female and Male, 18-20, non-workers)

Unfortunately, most of these benefits have a 'flip side'. Confidence can become arrogance, impulsiveness can become recklessness, saying what you think could offend somebody, and friendliness can be directed towards the wrong people. As with getting drunk itself, there is a 'thin line' that can be easily crossed. As we shall see in the next section, drunken offending, disorder and risk-taking often occur at this point.

I'd say the worst thing and a good thing is confidence, because you get confident and then you might get too confident and go and tell someone what you really think of them
                                                                    (Female, 18-20, non-worker)

A few young people described feeling as though they are 'in a bubble' when they are drunk. As their sense of self and enjoyment of the moment increases, their awareness of what is happening around them and the consequences of their actions diminishes.

People say, "Saw you out last Friday night", and it's almost like, "Did you?"... It's like you've had a couple of rounds and you don't realise what's going on around you. You live for the moment
                                                            (Female, 20-25, non-manual worker)

The best thing is it just makes you happy and the worst thing is you just don't care
                                                                    (Female, 18-20, non-worker)

Some young people admitted that they are likely to get argumentative or aggressive when they have been drinking. Many said the mood that they are in before they start drinking is the deciding factor in whether or not they get aggressive. They argued that getting drunk to try and 'take your mind off things' is a bad idea, as drink just exaggerates bad moods. Others said that particular drinks are more likely to make them aggressive. The drinks cited varied from person to person, although spirits (particularly vodka) and certain brands of lager were mentioned most often.

I think drink tends to make you paranoid. If someone just glances past you then you think they are staring at you and then you can just start for no reason at all
                                                                    (Male, 21-24, non-worker)

If you have got something in your head then don't drink, because you don't stop thinking about it and before you know it you are taking it out on someone
                                                                    (Male, 18-21, student)

Both men and women said that alcohol sometimes made them aggressive. The tendency to get aggressive, particularly in physical terms, was perceived by many young people of both sexes to be stronger in men. However, a few examples were given that contradicted this argument.

I think that men are more violent on drink, girls are a lot more chilled out

I have a drink and I just want to fight anyone   (Females, 21-24, non-worker)

Other negative consequences that young people mentioned involved damaging themselves physically when drunk; drunken accidents and incidents of alcohol poisoning were reported. As discussed in Chapter 2, young people's attitudes to these accidents varied; while most found them worrying, they were often reported with a degree of bravado.

> I woke up and I was in hospital... I had eight times the limit in my blood system, I had so much alcohol in my system and they were really worried. As soon as I went outside I hit the floor. That was eventful (Female, 18-20, non-worker)

Young people reported finding it difficult to judge their limits when it came to drinking (see Chapter 2). Alcohol blurred their *judgement* further by affecting their emotional, mental and physical reactions to events, often leading them into unexpected situations. As well as consumption levels and knowing their limits in terms of alcohol tolerance, it seems likely that age-specific factors will be relevant here, with lack of experience affecting their ability to judge situations.

Drugs versus drink

Those who used drugs were likely to say that the effects are more desirable than drinking. Cannabis in particular was viewed by many as safer than drinking. Harder drugs were not necessarily seen as safer in health terms. However, they were viewed by some as 'better' than alcohol because they provide a more reliable high, and were perceived as less likely to make people become aggressive, lose control of their actions, or forget what they have done the next morning.

> You are always in your right mind [with dope], with alcohol you are gone
> (Female, 18-20, non-worker)

> There is not much to do except going out and getting intoxicated, that is what people do at the end of the week... If there was somewhere to smoke, or whatever, then they wouldn't all wind up getting drunk and having a fight (Male, 18-20, non-manual worker)

Conclusions

The positive effects of binge drinking that the young people described relate closely to the motivations for binge drinking described in Chapter 2. Being drunk gives them social confidence, makes them feel happier about themselves and the world around them, and provides an escape from everyday routines by making them more adventurous and impulsive.

However, the young people were well aware of a more negative side to this change in mood and behaviour. There appear to be four main types of negative outcome identified, although these are closely related: *over-confidence* and *recklessness*, which encourage people to act in ways that they would normally consider unwise or inappropriate, *lack of awareness*, where people are too drunk to be fully aware of what is happening around them and to judge a situation accordingly, and *aggression*, which many young people said was more likely if they were in a bad mood when they started drinking. These factors, along with the physical effects of alcohol, can *blur judgement*, causing young people to behave in ways they would not wish to when sober. In extreme cases, such as those involving accidents or alcohol poisoning, complete *loss of control* can occur.

Some young people believed particular types of drink were more likely to make them aggressive, with spirits being mentioned most often. This recalls Cookson's (1992) finding of a significant association between violent offences and excessive consumption of spirits in her sample of young offenders. The more negative consequences of drinking were cited by some recreational drug users as a reason for preferring drugs; they were thought to be safer than alcohol or more reliable in their effects.

The impact of binge drinking on mood and behaviour forms a crucial part of the context in which crime and disorder on a night out takes place, as well as helping to explain young people's motivations for binge drinking. The 'model' of binge drinking proposed in this report aims to show how the more negative effects on individuals can combine with features of the broader social and environmental context to make crime and disorder in the night-time economy more likely.

A key element of this project was to explore the effects of drinking alcohol on young people's behaviour, with a particular emphasis on disorder and risk-taking. Groups were initially recruited according to three categories: those who had committed an offence or shown disorderly behaviour while drunk; those who had been the victim of an offence while drunk; and those whose reported behaviour characterised them as either 'at risk', or in neither of the aforementioned categories. However, as anticipated, it soon became apparent that these distinctions were not exclusive. For instance, while non-workers in one area were recruited as 'victims', the discussion was lead largely by their offending behaviour. What is more, in many cases a single incident could be classified in more than one way. Indeed, one of the key findings of the research was the frequency and rapidity with which the boundaries between risk-taking, being a victim and offending can be crossed.

For the most part, the young people appeared to be comfortable discussing their drunken experiences. While the attitudes displayed to the different offending and risk types often varied both within and between groups, on the whole they felt that more extreme behaviour while drunk was only to be expected. Drunkenness was often viewed as an acceptable excuse for people's more worrying actions; it seems likely that people were a lot happier discussing drunken misbehaviour than they might have been discussing sober misbehaviour.

Some of the types of **risk behaviour** that young people have undertaken while drunk can be summarised as:

- unprotected sex or sex with someone they did not know;
- walking home alone at night through areas they would not normally go when sober, such as through a dark park;
- getting in a car with a stranger or going back to a stranger's house;
- getting into a car with someone who is drunk;
- the use of unlicensed mini cabs; and
- pranks that put them in physical danger, e.g. climbing up buildings.

In addition, the **disorderly behaviour**, or offending, which young people in the research admit to can be briefly summarised as:

- fighting, leading in some cases to serious injury;
- prank or 'trophy' thefts, e.g. stealing items such as ashtrays from pubs, bars and night-clubs, or pieces of 'street furniture' such as traffic cones, road signs and bollards;
- other prank offences or vandalism, e.g. turning over bins, obstructing traffic; and
- other random offences, such as stealing a taxi, not paying a taxi fare, etc.

Offences young people had been a **victim** of were:

- fighting, leading in some cases to serious injury;
- rape, sexual assault and sexual harassment; and
- theft from the person.

Risk-taking behaviour

Many of the young people we spoke to did not perceive that they had put themselves at risk unless something unpleasant had actually happened to them. They often found it difficult to think of situations they had got into while drunk which could have had a harmful or dangerous conclusion. During the discussions, however, the young people gave numerous examples of risky situations which they had been involved in as part of a night out. These were often accepted as commonplace features of a drinking session, until the discussion encouraged them to reflect on the potential dangers involved.

Some risks were taken primarily out of a sense of necessity. These included walking home alone or through areas where they would not normally walk at night, and taking unlicensed cabs. These were generally seen as being more risky for women than for men. While the young women recognised that they should avoid putting themselves in compromising situations at the end of a night's drinking, they felt that this was not always possible. Indeed, a few argued that it was best to ignore concerns about being vulnerable, as these could interfere with their personal choices and stop them from having the confidence to go out and about as they wish to.

The majority, however, described drunkenness as a factor in their risk-taking alongside necessity and personal choice. Alcohol was described as affecting their judgement by encouraging reckless behaviour and a feeling of invulnerability. Most young people acknowledged that although they might *feel* invulnerable while drunk, being drunk actually made them more vulnerable to other people. This is both because others are more likely to take advantage of drunk people, and because drunk people are likely to be less suspicious of others.

I always feel I am in control of myself when I am drunk, and I don't think I am wasted because I am drunk. But at the time you think, "This is OK, I've thought this through…" So you are more likely to think this isn't going to end in a bad way. It clouds your judgement of [a situation], but you do think at the time that it's OK (Female, 18-21, student)

People, if they see you drunk they take the piss out of you. They take advantage, they know they are going to get the better of you (Male, 18-20, manual worker)

That said, there were some who argued that even by going out one is at risk, and there is little difference between being drunk or sober. In the same way as one is at risk when crossing the road or driving a car in broad daylight, any incident could occur in the evening while out and about.

You can get run over when you are sober. There is no difference when you are pissed (Male, 18-20, manual worker)

The following subsections explore the risk-taking behaviours that were discussed in the groups, and the influence of binge drinking in these incidents.

Getting home

Most of the groups, with the exception of the all-male groups, discussed the problems involved in getting home after a night's drinking. Situations that were seen as potentially risky were: walking home alone or walking down dark alleyways, using unlicensed mini-cabs and accepting lifts from strangers. These issues were discussed overwhelmingly in terms of the risk they could pose for women. Indeed, most of the risks for women were perceived to be on the way home.

Unlicensed mini cabs were perceived as posing a considerable threat to young women's safety. There were several accounts of threatening behaviour, and potential sex risks.

A cab driver tried to touch me up and kissed me as I was getting out of the cab, and I just pushed him back and got out of the cab and ran out of the stairs to home. I was a bit freaked out by that really (Female, 21-24, student)

I had to get a cab back by myself and I got in and I was completely gone… I sat there, then he locked the car doors… And I thought, "What are you doing?"… I said, "I have my mobile phone and I have 999 on it and all I have to do is press on it" (Female, 21-24, student)

Some young people reported that when they were impatient to get home after a night out, their impatience could combine with drunken impulsiveness to cause risky situations. Several described getting lifts with strangers, or with drunk friends.

> We were on the way to the black cab stands, and [a friend] stopped two of his friends driving this car, and he said, "What way are you going, can you drop these two off?", and we were like, "Yes, that will save us a bit of money"... The next morning my mate came around, and she went, "Have you seen that car? It is all smashed up outside"
>
> (Female, 18-20, non-worker)

In these situations, being drunk made them less aware of the potential consequences of their actions, and more single-mindedly determined to achieve their immediate aim, which was usually to get home. In some cases, young people were simply too drunk to realise the dangers. In others, the confidence inspired by drinking encouraged them to turn a blind eye to the risks.

> There is no way on earth you would get in [sober]. But when you are drunk you think that you are invincible, it is like nothing
>
> You are cold, you are hungry and you are tired, so you just think, "Oh, I just have to get home"
>
> (Females, 18-20, non-manual workers)

Risks taken while walking home were also an issue. While many young women said that they would not consider walking alone after dark under any circumstances, those who did walk alone often did not recognise this as a risk until they were prompted to do so. Some said they could not understand the risks involved as they had always been safe so far, while others, particularly those who lived alone, said they could not allow themselves to feel that way without compromising their freedom to go out.

> I've been attacked once when I was coming back from a club. It was only a short walk... I always walk with a friend now
>
> (Female, 18-20, student)
>
> I don't think walking home on my own is dangerous, because I can't allow myself to think like that at all. And I like to go out (
>
> Female, 21-24, student)

Continuing the party

Going back to a strange person's house in order to carry on drinking was another common theme. While several young women recognised these situations as risky during the group discussions, they said that their desire to keep on drinking and enjoying the night means that they often refuse to consider the more negative possibilities at the time. However, it was also the case that many of the young women did not wish to exaggerate the risks that they face. They wanted to feel free to move around as they chose, tended to feel safe when they were with a group of friends, and did not necessarily want to assume the worst about everybody.

> *I used to be at the University and during the summer lots of groups of men came and stayed in our area, we used to go back to the hotel rooms and get absolutely legless with them*   (Female, 20-24, manual worker)

> *Meeting people, "So-and-so is having a party back at his, do you want to go?" And like fair enough there are a couple of your mates with you, but you go back, but you have no idea what is actually waiting for you when you get there. And I am not saying that everyone is dodgy or anything*   (Female, 18-20, manual worker)

One night stands and unprotected sex

In most groups there was some discussion around the issue of 'one night stands'. Both men and women agreed that alcohol gives them confidence, and makes it easier to talk to people of the opposite sex. While this was a good thing if it enabled them to approach those they found attractive, many felt that alcohol made them less discriminating in their choices.

> *You could go for someone who is completely not your type, but you don't care because you are drunk*

> *In a way it's a good thing, for people who don't often get girlfriends for one reason or another*   (Females, 18-20, non-workers)

Experiences of drunken one night stands varied. Some involved making a conscious choice, albeit one that the young person might not have made if sober, while in other cases people had woken up in a strange bed or next to a strange person with no idea of how they had got there. Some young people were disturbed by the experience of waking up next to a stranger, while others displayed a more flippant attitude. This difference in approach recalls a similar range of attitudes discussed in Chapter 2; some young people are worried about 'losing control' when drunk, while others view incidents such as memory loss as part of the fun and adventure of a big night out. The young women in the groups tended to express more serious reservations about their one night stands than the young men, although this did not necessarily stop them from doing the same thing again later on.

I am drunk, but at the time you think "This is okay, I've thought it through and he's a really nice bloke" (Female, 18-21, student)

I just didn't know what happened, didn't know how I had got home, didn't know what I had done with that guy, it was a mess (Female, 18-20, non-manual worker)

Unsafe sex is clearly an issue here, with some of the drunkest saying that they were unable to remember whether they had taken precautions or not. More generally, a few young people said that getting drunk made them more likely to 'get carried away' and ignore the issue of contraception and STDs, even when they were fully aware of what they were doing. Again, it tended to be the women who are were concerned about the lack of protection during sex. A few of the men, particularly those in the all-male groups, expressed little or no concern.

You don't seem to care, whereas if you were sober you know [unprotected sex] *wouldn't happen* (Female, 20-24, manual worker)

Young people who had not taken these risks were likely to argue that being drunk was 'no excuse'. Those who had been careless about contraception after alcohol were less certain of this, and gave some ambiguous responses as to whether it was drink or other factors that allowed them to get 'carried away'. However, comments made by several of them did seem to suggest that alcohol prompted them towards the more reckless extreme of behaviour that they might consider anyway, rather than producing behaviour that was totally out of character. It is interesting to note that even among young people who had taken the same risks, there were differences of opinion as to whether alcohol could be considered as the cause of their behaviour or a viable 'excuse' for it. These contrasting views, which were also evident in the discussions of offending behaviour, suggest some significant differences in attitudes towards and experiences of alcohol among this age group.

Everyone knows it, if you are sober enough to get it up, then you must have some control (Male, 18-21, student)

I tend to forget to use a condom, just completely forget... Oh yes, a lot more [when I'm drunk]. *But it still happens sometimes, it depends but the risk is there* (Female, 18-20, student)

Disorder

Although young people's personal experience of disorder in the night-time economy varied, the relationship between binge drinking and disorder was acknowledged in all of the discussions. Fighting was the type of disorder mentioned most frequently, and was the main topic of conversation in the all-male groups. Most of the young men had some experience of drunken fights, although for the majority this was not something which happened to them regularly. Several of the young women had also been in fights, although once again these tended to be occasional rather than regular incidents.

For many, fighting while drunk was seen to be a 'fact of life', inevitable in situations where young people are drinking. This was particularly the case among those who were more often involved in this type of behaviour. As with risk-taking in the previous section, there were some who took the fatalistic view that these incidents are unavoidable.

It is part of the way of life

It is part of our heritage. Like football matches, you always get a fight at the end
(Males, 18-20, manual workers)

It is a shame that it has to be like that but that is the way it is. You are not going to change it at all, there are always going to be blokes like that. You have to do your best to avoid them really
(Male, 18-20, non-manual worker)

Most of the groups discussed the issue of fighting, although this was generally considered to be more of an issue for young men. Arguments and fights were described as usually starting over insignificant incidents, most commonly between people who do not know each other.

You'd be dancing on the dance floor and someone would push past you, you know, jab you. I'd jab them back... They do it so many times and then you just get so banged up... and that's when I attack back. End up on the floor, pulling your hair and stuff
(Female, 18-20, student)

He tried to chat up my girlfriend in front of me and I told him to piss off, so he said let's go outside
(Male, 18-20, non-worker)

While few of the young people interviewed said that they would go out 'looking' for a fight, many argued that there are others who do. Some felt that drunken fights were caused mainly by the overall personality of the fighters, rather than by the drink itself. The argument here seems to be that alcohol gives you confidence, but only the confidence to do the things that you would like to do anyway. As with unprotected sex, many young people clearly regarded alcohol as 'no excuse' for violence.

For some people [fighting] *is the ambition of the night, isn't it?* (Male, 21-24, non-worker)

At the end of the day it all comes down to the character of the person, because if you are violent and you have got a drink inside you, you are just going to explode
(Male, 18-21, student)

In some of the discussions, particular social groups were described as having a tendency towards violence. For example, one group identified the "Ben Sherman shirt brigade" as the people most likely to start fights in their city centre, and another said that fights in their town were usually caused by the traveller community. Young people like these seem to be saying that different 'types' of people cause drunken violence; once again, the argument is that alcohol only exaggerates the anti-social tendencies of anti-social people. There is a degree of contradiction here, however, as several young people who made these arguments about 'others' also admitted to starting fights on a night out themselves. When young people considered their own aggressive behaviour, they were more inclined to admit that alcohol can make a decisive difference by exaggerating emotions and shortening the distance between thought and action.

You feel like you can take on the world when you are pissed, that is the thing
(Male, 18-21, student)

Certainly many of those who had not been in fights as such described themselves as becoming more aggressive towards family or friends while drunk. For those who had got into fights while drunk, experiences seem to be divided into those where alcohol appears to exaggerate people's violent impulses and give them more confidence to act on them, and those where the fighter's behaviour appears to be more seriously 'out of control'.

I was really drunk and my boyfriend was annoying me chronically, thinking I was flirting with every single guy in the place, and he just annoyed me so much I hit him. I don't know why, because I am not that sort of person (Female, 18-20, non-manual worker)

I woke up in a police cell and I didn't know what had happened. I went to court and they read out what had happened and I was shocked. They said that I kicked four coppers in the balls   (Male, 21-24, non-worker)

While many of the drunken fighters had serious regrets next day, some of those who were more in control of their decision to fight felt able to stand by their decision even after they had sobered up, and did not see the drink as being ultimately responsible for their actions. Those who were more out of control sometimes tried to abdicate responsibility by saying that they 'weren't themselves' – here again we see the view that alcohol is an acceptable excuse for anti-social behaviour.

The next day I feel really bad, I shouldn't have done that, that person didn't deserve that   (Female, 21-24, non-worker)

I was on cocktails all day long and then drinking shots and stuff, I just knew that it wasn't me when I just went at him and started biting his chest. It was crazy
(Male, 18-21, student)

Although most young people argued that they would only fight under duress, there was a wide range of views as to what constitutes acceptable provocation for a fight. Some would only hit back if they were hit first, while others considered being insulted or pushed as grounds for 'starting'. The majority said that whatever their personal 'threshold' of tolerance is, being drunk is likely to lower it. In an environment where drink is making some people clumsy and others aggressive or paranoid, this makes misunderstandings and arguments more likely.

There is the three hit rule… If they hit you more than three times you are allowed to belt them one   (Male, 18-20, non-worker)

If someone is mouthy to you in a pub and you've had a few drinks then you're more likely to do something about it   (Male, 21-24, non-worker)

The young people who appeared less tolerant were often unwilling to consider themselves as victims, and said that they would feel obliged to stand up for themselves or their mates in a tricky situation. In some cases, this leads to an ambiguous situation where a person becomes the aggressor in order to avoid the perceived risk of being made a victim.

I have come up with the idea that I am not going to wait to be hit anymore, as it is just stupid standing there saying, "Look, mate, no, no", and you know what is going to happen, and you are going to be the one left bleeding

(Male, 21-24, non-manual worker)

[I start on people] *in case they get to me first* (Female, 21-24, non-worker)

While aggression and alcohol were perceived as the key ingredients in fighting, other factors were also involved. Friendship groups often played a key part. Some young people reported feeling obliged to join in with a fight in order to support their friends, while others felt more confident to start fights if they knew that the friends they are with are likely to back them up. Large groups of young men were seen as particularly likely to get involved in 'gang fights' where everybody joins in. Aggressive girls were more likely to describe being goaded towards violence verbally by friends.

You're a group of boys, you see another group of boys, "Let's have a war"

(Male, 18-20, student)

Some friends will go, "You are not going to stand for that, are you going to let her talk to you like that? Knock her out, silly bitch" (Female, 21-24, non-worker)

I have got a friend by the side of me and she is saying, "Look what she is wearing, the little slut", and all that (Female, 18-20, manual worker)

The crowded environment of pubs and night-clubs was described by some as encouraging violence, and aggressive bouncers were often blamed for aggravating the situation. However, most people recognised that the majority of the violence occurs on the streets after closing time.

When they won't let you in, that is what causes half the fuss with the bouncers anyway. Kids that have already had a drink then get stroppy

(Male, 18-20, manual worker)

I must admit most of the fights I've seen have been out in the streets, they weren't actually in the pubs (Male, 18-20, non-worker)

The frustration that is felt by revellers who have been forced outside before they are ready and the difficulties they may experience getting in somewhere else or finding a taxi home were often described as the key 'triggers' of violence. The crowded streets, and the fact that this is the point when people are at their most drunk, were also viewed as playing a part. A further factor, particularly relevant in areas where there are strong social tensions between groups, is the fact that this point of the evening may bring different types of drinker who frequent different venues together.

> *At 11pm everyone just piles out onto the street... Most people probably only went out at about 9pm... So they are just getting into it and then they are thrown out, they haven't had time to slow themselves down or anything* (Male, 18-21, student)

> *If it's raining people are pissed, they just want to get home... You see problems between people, "This is my taxi, I got it first", kind of thing*
> (Female, 18-21, student)

> *There are too many different things on the same night, so you get all sorts of different people out and it's all in the same area... Everyone comes out and there's only one road to go down and that's where it'll all start* (Male, 21-24, manual worker)

Several groups perceived their town centre as being quite a violent place, making fights more difficult to avoid. In the smaller towns this was often exacerbated by the lack of places to go after closing time, and the fact that everyone goes to the same place to start their journey home. For two of the all-male groups, the drinking environment appeared to be particularly violent, with drunken fights in some cases being related to broader patterns of offending and disorder in the area.

> *If someone is doing something, like a car stereo, everyone always has a fight after. Everyone is battering and scrapping* (Male, 18-20, manual worker)

> *Until I moved to [town name] I'd never broke a bone in my body, but in one year I've broken my arm around six times and I've broken all my fingers, [and] my collar bone has been snapped* (Male, 21-24, non-worker)

Drunken pranks

Depending on their precise nature, drunken pranks may fall into either the risk-taking or offending behaviour categories (or in some cases, both at once). Drunken pranks are included in the 'Disorder' section of this study as it concentrates on the more extreme type of prank; however, the young people themselves often did not recognise their 'pranks' as an offence.

Drunken pranks were more common among the young men. These frequently involved a show of bravado in front of friends, and many were potentially very dangerous. Several young women had also carried out some outlandish pranks when encouraged by their friends, although the women were less inclined to risk physical harm to themselves. Drunken pranks often involved traffic, while other 'dares' were also evident.

> It was on the national news and everything, as we basically caused a massive traffic jam in the centre of town. Because there were no traffic lights, just baskets of flowers which we'd hung   (Male, 21-24, non-manual worker)

> One time it was really, really funny, because they had cordoned off the market place with traffic cones. So we took all the traffic cones out of the market place and blocked the roads off with them   (Female, 18-20, manual worker)

Young people who reported these sorts of activities generally regarded them as harmless fun, and the potential consequences were only recognised in the cold light of day. The activities were associated with some of the positive effects of alcohol: becoming more playful, impulsive, adventurous and easily amused. Although some of the more extreme pranks might be described as quite disruptive or perhaps even destructive in nature, the young people themselves did not take this view. The young people described having no regrets the next morning, and did not appear to view themselves as 'offenders' or feel that they had 'lost control'.

> We thought it was absolutely hilarious... We thought we were the funniest people on the planet with these traffic cones   (Female, 18-20, manual worker)

Pranks which involved risk to the self, such as climbing statues or scaffolding and dodging cars in the road, were discussed in five of the groups. Both sexes reported this type of activity, although it appeared to be more common among men than women.

> There is a statue of a bloke on a horse, I have climbed up there. That is always good fun   (Male, 18-20, non-manual worker)

> I tried to climb over this really huge fence, with these huge spikes, at the top of my friend's house   (Female, 18-20, manual worker)

These sorts of prank were often taken more seriously, as they involved a risk of personal injury. Young people who had taken these risks said that alcohol seriously distorted their judgement of the situation, making them feel that they could 'do anything'. In some cases, people had hurt themselves or got themselves into tricky situations that they had to be rescued from.

They dragged me off at the end, because I was like going, at the top I was thinking, I don't know which way I am going to fall but I'm going to fall on them spikes
(Female, 18-20, manual worker)

Drinkers who had done this sort of thing were more likely to feel that they were 'out of control' at the time, and to be scared when they thought about the potential consequences. Their views were often similar to those of people who have damaged themselves in other ways by 'going too far' while drunk, such as hurting themselves by tripping and falling or ending up in hospital having their stomach pumped. Again concerns about the potential danger were combined with bravado and a desire to show off about their experience – the same motivations that prompted many of the pranks in the first place. Young people who had these experiences often belonged to the significant minority who felt that it was fun to lose control while drinking; while acknowledging the dangers, they regarded these escapades as part of the adventure of a night out.

When I like actually got off the wall and looked down I absolutely shat myself, like "What are you doing?" That is probably the worst thing I have ever done
(Male, 20-24, manual worker)

I have lost half a finger, and that is because I had too much to drink and I thought I had to get home quick so I climbed over a school fence (Male, 18-20, manual worker)

Alcohol was generally seen as the primary cause of pranks, with few people saying that their experience would have happened if they had been sober. As discussed above, drinking companions could also play an important role; young people were unlikely to do these sorts of things alone or without an audience. Comments made about being more open to suggestion when drunk indicate that young people are more likely to do this sort of thing when they are being encouraged by their friends. In the case of pranks that endanger the self, some suggested that a person's temperament can also make a difference; some young people are more inclined to show off, take foolish risks or be reckless than others.

Someone starts goading you into something... You are more likely to do it if someone is egging you on
(Male, 20-24, manual worker)

We were all like giving each other dares, and they said, "I bet you can't climb over that", and I was wearing a dress as well that I managed to rip, but I was like, "Yes I can"
(Female, 18-20, manual worker)

Experiences as a victim

Many of the incidents which led to a young person being subjected to an unpleasant, or sometimes criminal, situation have been discussed in both the risk and disorder sections. As discussed, young people were often unwilling to consider themselves to be 'at risk' through their activities while drinking. Consequently, those who had been victims were often described as being 'unlucky', and the exception rather than the norm.

Often these incidents were progressions of risks which had been taken on a night out, such as being raped after going back to a young man's house, attacked while coming home alone, harassed by a mini cab driver, or having things stolen after a one night stand.

I have been a fool with drink, I have been naïve, been back to somebody's place and was raped
(Female, 18-21, student)

The extent to which alcohol was held responsible for these episodes often depended on the degree of awareness a young person had when deciding whether to take a risk. In cases where memory loss is involved, events may be blamed entirely on a loss of control through drinking. In other situations alcohol is described as encouraging people to be less cautious, but is not held responsible for the entire scenario. In circumstances where the perpetrator was particularly aggressive, determined or 'out of control' themselves, young people sometimes argued that the situation would have remained the same had they been sober.

I think people can get into certain situations because they are drunk that they normally wouldn't put themselves in
(Female, 18-20, non-worker)

Someone could come up and beat you up anyway. You know it's got nothing to do with you being drunk, they could be drunk
(Male, 21-24, non-worker)

In the case of drunken fighting, it is often hard to distinguish between perpetrator and victim, particularly as the person who initially starts the fight may suffer the worst damage at the end. Those who got into fights when they were 'out of control' from drinking were less conscious of their actions, less aware of what was happening to them and more vulnerable to attack, which made the line between victim and offender still harder to draw.

After I had a fight I got battered, I had a fractured jaw and everything, and when I woke up there was a police officer there and he said, "You've been arrested". You know, I had to make my own way to the ****ing hospital, and I still got arrested
(Male, 21-24, non-worker)

Staying safe

The young people interviewed enjoyed drinking excessively, and described themselves as unlikely to change their drinking habits because of the possibility of getting into harmful situations. As discussed in previous sections, many took a rather fatalistic attitude to involvement in drunken disorder and risk.

You can't control that sort of thing, it just happens. You've got to know that sort of thing happens occasionally and you've got to accept it   (Male, 18-20, student)

However, most agreed that there are particular situations that can be avoided. Strategies for staying safe on a night out that were discussed in the groups included:

- **Pre-arranging mini cabs.** Young women in one all-female group said that they often pre-arranged mini cabs before going out at night, and asked to be picked up from wherever they were going. This was partly due to location and lack of suitable public transport, however, it would have been easy for them to put themselves at risk by using the unlicensed mini cabs. Instead, fuelled by either personal or recounted bad experiences, they tended to organise cabs from a company they were familiar with. Young people in smaller towns also tended to use firms they were familiar with; in areas like these this is often less of an issue as local taxi firms are easily accessible.

I order one before I leave, and then if I need to change it I just call them when I am there and just say, instead of picking me up at 3.00am, pick me up at this time instead. And then at least you know   (Female, 18-20, non-manual worker)

There are taxi places everywhere, everyone knows the numbers, so I don't think anyone would really [walk home]   (Female, 21-24, manual worker)

- **Avoiding 'trouble spots'.** Although more difficult in some of the localities which appear to have higher levels of offending generally, it is clear that there are often individual venues, or general areas, which tend to attract a 'hardcore' element. Therefore, in order to reduce risk these places could be avoided. In around half of the groups, people described doing this, often (although not exclusively) females, those in the older age bracket, and students.

It is safer to stay away from certain areas, you know (Male, 18-20, non-manual worker)

- **Sticking with friends.** Most of the young people felt that they could rely on their friends to prevent them from doing anything too foolish, and many stressed the importance of staying with people they could trust and not wandering off alone. However, the evidence suggests that this sense of security could be false in certain situations. A few stressed the importance of having friends to back them up in an argument, despite the fact that in several cases friends were described as aggravating violent situations and being more of a liability than a safety net.

I would never ever let one of my friends walk home on her own
(Female, 18-20, manual worker)

I think if you are in a group of girls you tend to be a bit safer   (Female, 21-24, student)

- **Staying calm.** As discussed above, there were several who argued that the best way of protecting yourself is by standing up for yourself, a position which when taken to extremes could lead to the view that 'the best form of defence is attack'. However, in most groups where these views were expressed there were people who took issue with them, emphasising the importance of staying calm, walking away and refusing to rise to provocation. Some former fighters cited age and life-stage as key factors in toning down their more aggressive attitudes.

I think if they are out for a fight they are going to pick on people that do answer back. It's easy enough just to walk away   (Male, 18-21, student)

A lot of friends have calmed down and had kids and bits and bobs like that... There is still that gang of friends, but everybody's sort of grown up and chilled out
(Female, 20-25, non-manual worker)

Conclusions

As suggested in Chapter 4, the effects of binge drinking on mood, behaviour and judgement are often closely related to young people's experiences of drunken disorder and risk-taking. In particular:

- **over-confidence** can encourage young people to think they are invincible, which can stop them from appreciating the risks attached to certain situations;
- **recklessness** also encourages them to act without considering the possible consequences;
- **lack of awareness or control** can be factors in cases where people are too drunk to know what they are doing or the situation they are in; and
- **aggression** may be stimulated by drunkenness, making people more likely to want to argue, pick a fight, or respond when provoked.

As discussed in Chapter 4, the positive and negative effects of binge drinking were viewed as closely linked, with the latter often perceived as being the 'flip side' of the former. While the negative effects of binge drinking were often seen as making drunken risk-taking and disorder more likely, some young people also associated the positive effects with disorderly outcomes. For example, some pranks were described as the result of drunken playfulness and not seen by those committing them as cause for concern. A few young people also discussed drunken fights as though they were something of a sport, rather than a serious issue. Although the latter was a minority view, episodes of disorder and risk were frequently seen as adventures, part of the excitement of getting drunk with friends.

The relationship between binge drinking and disorder is far from straightforward, however. Besides the effects of binge drinking themselves, there are many other factors which come into play when a binge drinking session has negative outcomes. Importantly, these factors are closely related to the social, attitudinal and environmental context within which binge drinking takes place, which means that the drivers of binge drinking itself may also be the drivers of risk-taking and offending behaviour while drunk. Also, as discussed in earlier chapters, many of the social and attitudinal influences on binge drinking behaviour among 18- to 24-year-olds are specific to their outlook, social position and lifestyle as young adults.

Key elements in the relationship between binge drinking and disorder among this age group include:

- **Desire to push the limits/unwillingness to consider limits.** As well as being associated with heavy drinking and (for some) mixing drink and drugs, this attitude may inform certain types of drunken risk-taking, such as a young person going back to a stranger's house because they want the night to continue for as long as possible. Furthermore, a significant minority of the young people thought it was fun disregard their limits and drink until they lost control; this group appeared more prone to a variety of disorderly and risk-taking behaviours.

- **Association of drinking with personal freedom or 'escape'.** Binge drinking is associated with a release from everyday worries. It may be this mindset that makes young people less inclined to consider the consequences of their actions, as well as the effects of the drinking binge itself. As discussed, many felt that the risks surrounding binge drinking should not be taken too seriously as this would curtail their freedom – particularly in the case of the young women. The young people often talked about disorderly or risky episodes in terms of excitement. This suggests that binge drinking may provide them with an 'escape' from everyday responsibilities as well as everyday routines, given them an excuse for reckless or anti-social behaviour. As we have seen, the belief that drunkenness is an acceptable excuse for misbehaviour is more common in some young people than others.

- **Peer group influence.** Friends were often described as 'egging each other on' to drink more, and in some cases also encouraged pranks, fights and other forms of risk-taking. As discussed in Chapter 3, many young people described themselves as behaving quite differently on a night out depending on the group of friends they were with. The sense of being 'in it together' can encourage reckless behaviour by promoting over-confidence or a false sense of security, and by making such behaviour seem more acceptable.

- **The environmental context.** Crowded venues, aggressive door staff and particularly 'rough' areas or premises were seen as increasing the likelihood of drunken fights. More generally, closing time was seen as the high point of the evening for trouble, particularly in towns where there was little available after 11 pm. Clashes over taxis and concerns about getting home indicate that lack of late-night transport can also cause problems. These findings echo those of several earlier research studies. The impact of crowding on the likelihood of violence in venues has been explored by McIntyre and Homel (1997), while Marsh and Kibby (1992) have drawn attention to the concentration of alcohol-related violence between 11 pm and midnight on a Friday and Saturday. Wells et al., (1998) have explored the crucial role of bouncers in aggressive incidents, dividing their responses into the 'good' (preventing or minimising violence), the 'bad' (unfair, inconsistent, delayed or poorly judged) and the 'ugly' (aggressive, hostile or provocative).

- **Social attitudes.** As discussed in Chapter 3, tensions between different social groups within the night-time economy often affected young people's perceptions of who the troublemakers are. Most were alert to the possibility of trouble on a night out, with a few determined to stand their ground at all costs. For some, perceptions or prior experience of other young drinkers had made them defensive enough to adopt the view that 'the best form of defence is attack'. This recalls research findings that stress the importance of *expectations* in fuelling violence among drinkers (Brown *et al.*, 1980; Graham *et al.*, 1998; Turning Point, 1998).

6   Controlling the crowd: interventions and messages

One purpose of the research is to inform the development of policies aimed at promoting sensible drinking and reducing the social harms associated with binge drinking. In view of this, the young people were asked to suggest any approaches that they felt might be effective. The improvements discussed have been divided into two broad categories. These are *interventions*, which aim to change the drinking environment in order to make it safer for drinkers, and *messages*, which aim to change the attitudes and behaviour of individuals through advertising.

The main **interventions** suggested and discussed by the young people were:

- changes to the licensing laws to extend drinking hours, with some young people suggesting '24 hour' drinking venues;
- providing a greater range of places where young people could either drink or hang out 'after hours' (i.e. after 11.00 pm when the pubs close or after 2.00 am when the majority of night-clubs and 'late licence' bars close);
- increasing police presence outside bars, pubs, and night-clubs, particularly in known 'trouble spots';
- more intervention, or more effective forms of intervention, from the bouncers in pubs, bars and night-clubs;
- use of plastic glasses and bottles to lessen the risk of injury in fights; and
- improved public transport for people coming home from a night out.

The main points raised in relation to messages were:

- the difficulty of influencing people's drinking behaviour through advertising, particularly younger people who may interpret 'safer drinking' campaigns as 'lectures';
- the value of 'shock advertising' in making an impression on people;
- the importance of portraying real people in life-like scenarios, which makes young people more likely to relate the messages to themselves;
- the possibility that messages might have more of an impact if they are put across in the actual drinking environment, although there was disagreement about the value of this approach; and
- the need for more balanced long-term initiatives alongside 'shock' campaigns, in order to raise young people's overall awareness of the issues.

Changing the environment: policy interventions

Most young people favoured changing the licensing laws so that pubs, bars and night-clubs could stay open for longer. There were two main arguments given for this. Firstly, young people argued that prolonged drinking time would allow people to decide for themselves when their night was over, and to leave 'in their own time'. This would avoid one of the problems perceived as contributing to drunken fights, which was large numbers of annoyed customers leaving venues at the same time and clashing with each other at taxi ranks, in night-club queues, or in the street.

It would stagger it. Some people want to go home at midnight, other people want to stay out until 4pm (Female, 18-21, student)

It's like at 11pm you kick every single person that is in a pub out and get a mass influx of drunk people out, and if you have people coming out in dribs and drabs you might not get the big fights (Female, 21-24, non-manual worker)

The second argument was that longer licensing hours would encourage people to slow the pace of their drinking, which would give them more control over how drunk they get and make extreme behaviour less likely. Some young people perceived European countries as places where drinking behaviour is less extreme than in England, and felt that longer licensing hours were the ultimate cause of this difference.

They're not going to be in such a mad rush to get absolutely smashed before 11pm (Male, 21-24, non-worker)

That is why British holidaymakers have such a bad reputation, because they go off and drink as quickly as possible in the shortest amount of time because they are not used to the club being open until 6am. They could pace themselves and have a good time (Female, 21-24, student)

The second argument was given slightly less frequently than the first one, and some young people were not entirely convinced. While many suggested that longer drinking hours would lead to the same amount of alcohol being consumed more slowly, a few felt that longer hours might actually encourage immoderate drinking, as some people would not know when to stop. This reflects the perceptions that several young people had of their own drinking habits; as discussed in Chapter 2, many found it hard to know their limits and judge when it was time to moderate their drinking.

Instead of having 12 pints in three hours, you can have 12 pints in five hours, so you're not going to be as pissed (Male, 21-24, non-worker)

If it is open longer people are going to end up getting even more drunk, and maybe cause even more trouble (Female, 20-24, manual worker)

On the whole, the young people were very supportive of the idea of longer licensing hours, but as the more doubtful comments indicate, they perceived a potential for some negative effects alongside the benefits.

As well as new licensing laws, some young people proposed that there should be a greater range of late-night licensed venues available to give them an alternative to going home after the pubs had closed. This was felt particularly strongly in areas where there were only a few night-clubs or bars that were open past 11.00 pm. Some young people are not keen to continue an evening out in a night-club, particularly when they need to pay to get in. A few argued that young people needed quieter venues to go to after a pub or night-club. These places would not necessarily need to sell alcohol, and could give young people a space in which to 'wind down' and sober up after their big night. Some of these young people felt that there should be more alternatives to drinking generally for young people who want to socialise, or related their argument to the case for legalising cannabis.

Maybe the alcohol's served only until 2am, but there's something there longer... Have a game of pool and then they go home. Just more places that are a bit more friendly. Let you in, chill you out (Female, 20-25, non-manual worker)

Another option of being able to go and smoke dope or something, another place to go as you can't go anywhere else (Male, 21-24, non-manual worker)

Increasing the police presence in town centres was generally viewed as a positive move, as it would increase the chances of fights being dealt with immediately. This was seen as a particularly good idea outside venues or in parts of town that were known as 'trouble spots'. Some argued that the current police presence on their nights out was ineffective, as the police did not take drunken violence seriously; it was felt that these attitudes needed to be challenged.

You can ask anyone in a town or city and they will name you the bad places, they should know these places and they should keep an eye on them. Hang around outside all these pubs and clubs and stuff that are going to cause trouble at 11pm when all the troublemakers spill out (Male, 21-24, manual worker)

If you're drunk the police just steer round you if you're in trouble

(Female, 18-20, student)

A few young people, particularly young men, argued that having more police on the streets would actually aggravate trouble as it would antagonise young people on a night out. A few believed that people who were drunk and determined to fight might find it easy to ignore the police. However, many young people who had been in fights themselves argued that a greater police presence would certainly discourage *them* from causing trouble. Indeed, it was interesting to find that even young people who had started fights, been in fights regularly or been in trouble with the police on a 'big night out' were often in favour of increasing the police presence. This reflects the finding that the line between victim and offender is often blurred in drunken fights; those who are aggressive may also need protection.

Half the time the police on the street is what causes the fight anyway. People are fed up with seeing the cops   (Male, 18-20, manual worker)

*It is good really, because if the police weren't there then you would get ****ed*

(Male, 18-21, student)

Bouncers were often perceived as playing a part in aggravating violence, although young people's perceptions of their role varied. Some criticised them for being too aggressive about their duties, saying that they are likely to be abusive and to attack people who have done nothing wrong. Others said that they are too passive about stopping trouble, and that instead of intervening in fights and splitting people up they will simply throw them off the premises and leave them to battle it out in the street. This is one reason why some of the young people suggested that a police presence directly outside particular pubs or night-clubs would be a good idea.

I saw this massive chap pick on this small guy, and then it was the small guy that was thrown out and he didn't start it   (Male, 18-20, non-manual worker)

They throw you out and then they throw the other geezers out and you are outside with these three geezers, and you are just stuck there and they are saying, "Do you want a fight?"... I think they should do something about that, really

(Male, 18-21, student)

Comments made about bouncers reflect a broader argument that some of the young people made in relation to drunken disorder; that pubs and night-clubs bear a responsibility for controlling the situation, and that it is not a matter for the police or individuals alone. Where young people identified crowded pubs and clubs as a factor which can aggravate tensions, this was sometimes perceived as a question of the businesses putting their profits before people. Furthermore, staff at pubs and clubs were seen as having the final say over who is allowed on the premises and who is allowed to keep on drinking.

> *The clubs are selfish because they just let so many people in. I went to a club a few*
> *months ago, it was so busy that you couldn't walk*
> (Female, 18-20, non-manual worker)

However, it was recognised that the town centre environment may be hard to police, as it is difficult to keep track of people when they are in a crowd and moving from place to place, and can be impossible to know in advance which people are likely to start trouble. A scheme in place in one large town, where a CCTV and radio link is used to pass information about trouble-makers from venue to venue, was given as an example of how different venues could co-operate with each other and with the police in order to keep control of the situation.

> *If we have someone in our pub who is kicking off, you get on there and you say,*
> *"This is so-and-so, wearing so-and-so, he has done this, this and this, could you*
> *please bar him from every pub in town"* (Female, 18-20, manual worker)

There were mixed views on whether plastic glasses or bottles could change the environment for the better. There was a general feeling that drinks served in plastic glasses would be irritating, and that a plastic pint glass would not feel like a 'real' pint. However, several argued that this was not really important and that the priority should be to prevent injuries.

> *Like being at a kid's party almost. You feel like you are being treated like a child*
> (Female, 20-25, non-manual worker)

> *It is horrible drinking a pint out of a plastic cup*

> *It might be horrible, but it could save your life one day* (Males, 18-21, students)

Many young people were aware of cases where people had been seriously injured by glass in a fight, and it was felt that plastic bottles and glasses could reduce such incidents. However, one group felt that the people who were likely to use bottles in fights would simply find themselves an alternative weapon. In addition, a few young people said that plastic glasses were easier to spill and therefore more likely to cause fights. It is worth noting that young people who were more used to drinking in venues with plastic glasses and bottles expressed more positive views, which suggests that such measures may grow in popularity once they have been introduced. Some other alternatives, such as shatterproof glass, were also mentioned.

You can get like proper plastic strong [cups], *they were handed out at student bashes... You could just chuck them away or be recycled, there wasn't smashed glass all over the floor. I don't know how much that would cost pubs and clubs to do. If it costs too much money they won't do it*   (Male, 21-24, manual worker)

A few of the groups mentioned improved late-night transport as part of the solution to the problems associated with binge drinking. The extent to which this was perceived as an issue seemed to depend on three factors: the distance between young people's homes and drinking venues, the availability and affordability of taxis, and the existing public transport provision.

If you want to be sure of getting a bus it has got to be 10.30pm, or otherwise you have to walk   (Male, 18-20, non-manual worker)

They have opened up late-night buses now... They've put about five on, and they've all got security guards. You don't get any trouble on them buses, and they go to all the roughest areas as well   (Male, 18-21, student)

Those in smaller towns and those who lived closer to the area they went out in were happier to rely on taxis. Those who were less happy with transport arrangements suggested a variety of improvements, including late-night buses, trams or trains, increased taxi provision, and a coach service to take people to and from particular drinking venues.

Changing peoples' attitudes: advertising messages

The overall view among the young people was that they liked to go out drinking, and that advertising campaigns were unlikely to change their behaviour significantly. Many felt that until something bad happened to themselves or somebody they knew, their inclination would be to consider themselves invulnerable and not worry about the risks involved in drinking heavily or in being part of the drinking environment.

The trouble is you think it is not going to happen to you.

I think they need to create more awareness that it does happen
(Females, 18-20, non-manual workers)

Some perceived this attitude as being an aspect of 'human nature' in general. Others related it to age, and said that being young made them less likely to worry about the more 'long-term' consequences of heavy drinking, such as the health risks.

People think they're immortal and I think it's their attitude, it's their mental thing, until you get it, and then when you get it it's too late, isn't it? (Male, 18-20, student)

Advertising campaigns were associated in many young people's minds with the 'lectures' they had from parents or teachers as teenagers, particularly for the younger people in the age group. There was a feeling that this sort of advice is bound to be ineffective; young people are naturally curious and often rebellious, which means that telling them not to do something can actually make them more inclined to do it. Once again, the stress was on young people finding out about the risks 'the hard way'.

Sitting there at school, all you want to do is rebel against it, you are being forced to wear things you don't want to wear, doing things you don't want to do. You go against it in any way you can (Female, 18-20, non-worker)

They have got to go through it themselves and learn from it
(Male, 18-20, manual worker)

Despite this overall perception, many young people had quite definite ideas about the sorts of advertising or messages that would be likely to have *more* of an impact on them. In most of the groups, young people argued that adverts with 'shock value' were the best way of getting messages about risk across. The drink driving adverts shown at Christmas, and the recent campaign encouraging back-seat passengers in cars to wear their seatbelts, were given as the best examples of this. Many young people stressed the importance of making these sorts of advertising campaigns as hard-hitting and 'gory' as possible, so that they would stick in people's minds.

It could be a girl being raped when she's drunk. It's got to be horrible. The sickest thing you can think of (Female, 18-20, non-worker)

It was felt that presenting people with life-like scenarios rather than facts and figures would increase young people's perception of the risks. Drunken injuries and people getting attacked or assaulted were seen by some as suitable for this sort of approach.

> *Like a campaign with a body in a hospital with his face opened up from a pint glass...that would make you think, "Oh, I wouldn't like to be hit with a glass"*

> *Nobody cares about numbers and that*   (Males, 18-21, students)

Young people also supported the idea of visual presentations relating to the harmful health consequences. For example, they suggested pictures comparing an alcoholic's liver with a healthy one.

> *With the disgusting liver, just put a big one up, catch people's attention. You don't look at it much if it's not disgusting*   (Female, 18-20, non-worker)

A few young people argued that they were not fully aware of the health aspects around binge drinking, although many claimed that they knew them but were not really worried by them. Information on the physical effects of binge drinking was not seen as something that would affect young people's drinking patterns in the short term, but some felt that being more aware of this might have an impact on their attitudes in the long term.

> *If they made the awareness of kidney failure and things like that related to alcohol more apparent, because that happened to my ex-boyfriend...*

> *As long as it says it can happen to anyone at any age, because otherwise you think, "Gosh, it won't happen to me, but it will in about five years"*
>   (Females, 20-24, manual workers)

Opinion was divided on the best medium for advertising campaigns. Some argued that it would be a good idea to put the message across in pubs, bars and clubs, by using posters or beer mats. Their argument was that it would be best to display the message in the context of the drinking environment, where it is immediately relevant, and that campaigns on television or radio would be forgotten once people were actually in the pub. Young women in particular mentioned pub toilets as a place where they would notice advertisements and give them some thought.

I think it is all very well advertising when you are sat at home watching your TV. It makes you feel bad and then you go out and get pissed anyway...

If you have seen the adverts [in the pub] *then it brings it home to you. You have had a few beers and then you remember when you see it on the beer mat*

(Males, 18-20, non-manual workers)

Others took the opposite view, arguing that once a person is in the pub getting drunk they will be unlikely to notice campaign messages or take them seriously. Young people who argued this often felt that television would be the best medium, particularly in cases where shocking visual imagery was seen as the key to a good campaign. Billboard advertisements and radio campaigns were also mentioned.

You are in the pub to have a good time, and you don't think about things like that

(Female, 21-24, student)

If they did like an ad on television, an advert, then, like, maybe, because you are seeing it. Whereas if it is in poster form they can't get really get that much across

(Female, 18-20, non-manual worker)

Although the young people emphasised 'shock tactics' as the best way of making an *immediate* impression, some also saw a role for more balanced, long-term initiatives, aimed at raising people's awareness of the issues. A few argued that school was the best place for communicating these sorts of messages, as this would allow the authorities to communicate with young people before drinking patterns become too established.

Upper school age, before it gets to that stage. Before you get the habit

(Female, 21-24, manual worker)

These people felt that education about alcohol at school could be improved; some recalled being taught quite a lot about the effects of illegal drugs at school, but not very much about alcohol. In the light of the points raised about the dangers of 'lecturing' young people, one group argued that the best educational campaigns would provide unbiased information about the risks and effects of alcohol, rather than actively advising young people not to drink. This approach, it was felt, would allow young people to weigh up all the factors involved before making their own decisions.

It's funny, because we got drug talks at our school but not drink talks

(Female, 20-25, non-manual worker)

"Why should you drink alcohol underage?" rather than, "Don't drink alcohol". Then they ask themselves that question… It leaves out the authority

(Male, 18-20, non-worker)

Conclusions

The young people argued that the most effective way of tackling alcohol-related disorder was by changing the drinking environment. Extended licensing laws and a greater range of late-night venues were suggested as ways of slowing the pace of drinking and reducing the crowds of drinkers who are all on the move at the same time. Young people were in favour of practical measures to ensure their safety, such as late-night transport, more targeted policing. They believed that venue owners and staff held some responsibility for regulating the situation, with several groups discussing the role of bouncers in preventing (or aggravating) violence. Many supported the use of plastic or shatterproof bottles and glasses in licensed premises, although there was some debate about this.

They felt that advertising campaigns would have less of an impact than policy interventions, as they considered themselves unlikely to change their levels of drinking and the attitudes associated with these. Young people often related these patterns and habits to their age and life-stage, arguing that they would be more likely to worry about the consequences of their drinking when they got older, and stressing the importance of learning the risks through personal experience. Despite their fervour for getting drunk, however, they were aware that alcohol is a powerful drug that can have unpleasant consequences, and suggested that communications which highlight this fact might stick in their minds if the messages were strong enough. While most believed that this would be unlikely to affect their behaviour in the short term, they felt it might raise their overall awareness of the risks associated with binge drinking.

The young people's views on policy interventions reinforce the findings from various studies. For example, a number of studies have drawn attention to the large proportion of violence in the night-time economy occurring in a relatively small number of 'trouble spots' (Homel *et al.*, 2001; Marsh and Kibby, 1992; Ramsay, 1982). Jeffs and Saunders (1983) found a programme of high-profile policing, agreed between the police and licensees, to be effective in reducing alcohol-related violence over one summer in an English seaside resort.

Shepherd *et al.*, (1990) observed that some of the most severe injuries resulting from bar fights were caused by broken glass or bottles being used as weapons, while the British Crime Survey indicates that around one in seven incidents of violence between strangers and one in ten incidents of violence between acquaintances in pubs or clubs involved a bottle or glass (Mattinson, 2001). Marsh and Kibby (1992) used their observations of the concentration of incidents between 11 pm and midnight to make the case for extended licensing hours.

Improved or mandatory training has been advocated for both bar staff (Russ and Geller, 1987) and licensees (Norton, 1998), in order to encourage responsible server practice, while a registration scheme has been suggested for doormen in order to ensure that venue owners are hiring responsible individuals (Deehan *et al.*, 2002).

More generally, there has been a shift in both research and policy terms towards a partnership approach, ensuring that the representatives of various local agencies work together with licensees and venue staff to tackle alcohol-related crime and disorder (see for example Deehan, 1999; Deehan *et al.*, 2002; Homel *et al.*, 2001). As we have seen, a local scheme that allowed bouncers to co-operate with police officers was mentioned by several young people as an example of good practice.

7   Moving forward – conclusions & implications

As discussed throughout this report, the relationship between alcohol consumption and crime and disorder is far from straightforward. More specifically, young people's experiences of offending, disorder and risk-taking in the night-time economy cannot be attributed to their pattern of 'binge' drinking alone.

This study began from the premise that it would be necessary to understand the 'social context' of binge drinking among young adults in order to explain how a night out can end in disorder. The conclusion of the research is that while the *effects of binge drinking* on mood and behaviour may play a considerable part in disorderly outcomes, other factors of the social context can have an equally important influence. These factors can be grouped into three key areas: the *attitude and motivations* that young binge drinkers bring to drinking, the *social and peer group norms* under which they operate, and features relating to the *drinking environment*. Factors relating to attitude, motivations and social and peer group norms are often related to the specific experiences, values and lifestyles common to this age group.

Clearly, each of these four elements plays a part in any night on the town for any young binge drinker. However, the majority of nights out and binge drinking sessions do not end in disorderly outcomes. The model overleaf attempts to identify the key 'risk factors' within each category. These 'risk factors' are factors that increase the likelihood of a young binge drinker being involved in crime or disorder (whether as a victim or perpetrator), or otherwise behaving so as to put themselves 'at risk'. Frequently, it is the interaction of different risk factors – particularly those from different 'arms' of the model – that leads to disorderly outcomes.

The following paragraphs discuss the risk factors in more detail, although the substance of each is explained fully in earlier chapters of the report.

- **Attitudes and motivations** towards binge drinking (see Chapter 2). As we have seen, the majority of the young people interviewed had a strong *desire to push the limits* on a big night out: practices such as mixing drinks and deliberately drinking quickly in order to get more drunk were common. However, many young people also said they had *difficulty judging their limits* and often found themselves getting more drunk on an evening out than they had originally intended. Although many were cautious about getting 'too drunk' in theory, the combination of these factors meant that this nonetheless often happened in practice. Meanwhile, there were a significant minority who thought that it was *fun to lose control*, taking a flippant attitude towards events such as illness, accidents and memory loss.

As discussed in the conclusion to Chapter 5, the fact that *drinking is linked to personal freedom or escape* can make young binge drinkers less likely to consider the consequences of their actions. For example, some of the young women were reluctant to consider the safety issues around getting home because this prevented them from feeling independent. Meanwhile, *relieving stress or anger* was identified by the young people themselves as a 'risky' motivation for binge drinking; it was felt that alcohol often serves to aggravate negative feelings rather than 'drowning sorrows'

- **Social and peer group norms** (see Chapters 3 and 5). Drinking companions were seen as a key influence on binge drinking behaviour, in terms of both the amount that was drunk and behaviour while drinking. Some young people had been goaded into fighting or pranks by their friends (*friends who encourage extreme behaviour*). More generally, *group overconfidence* could also encourage reckless behaviour by engendering a false sense of security. Another justification given for misbehaviour was the attitude among some young people that *drunkenness is an acceptable excuse* that mitigates an individual's responsibility for their actions.

Social tensions or prejudice between different groups sometimes encouraged confrontational situations, and could influence young people's perceptions of where to expect trouble and who to expect it from. Many young people were very alert to the possibility of confrontation, with some even prepared to pre-empt fights if necessary. Sometimes this attitude was related to perceptions about the likelihood of trouble; in other cases it grew from social norms about the need to 'stand up for yourself', or the obligation to stand up for friends. Even young people who normally avoided confrontation could end up getting involved in fights in order to protect friends (*standing up for friends or self*).

- **Effects of binge drinking** (see Chapter 4). As discussed previously, getting drunk sometimes led to *overconfidence, recklessness or impulsiveness, lack of awareness and aggression*. These and other ways in which alcohol *blurs judgement* could have negative consequences, including outcomes related to risk-taking, disorderly behaviour and becoming the victim of an offence (see Chapter 5). In more extreme cases binge drinking could lead to *loss of control*, as when young people had been involved in fights and could not remember afterwards how they had started.

Key risk factors

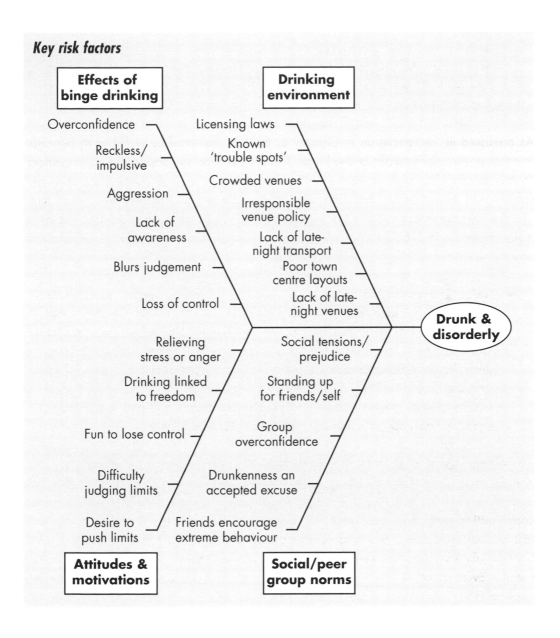

Effects of binge drinking

Overconfidence

Reckless/impulsive

Aggression

Lack of awareness

Blurs judgement

Loss of control

Relieving stress or anger

Drinking linked to freedom

Fun to lose control

Difficulty judging limits

Desire to push limits

Attitudes & motivations

Drinking environment

Licensing laws

Known 'trouble spots'

Crowded venues

Irresponsible venue policy

Lack of late-night transport

Poor town centre layouts

Lack of late-night venues

Social tensions/prejudice

Standing up for friends/self

Group overconfidence

Drunkenness an accepted excuse

Friends encourage extreme behaviour

Social/peer group norms

Drunk & disorderly

- **The drinking environment** (see Chapters 3 and 5). Young people were aware of *known 'trouble spots'* in their town, where they expected there to be fighting. As we have seen, expectations of violence can play a role in accelerating violence. More generally, young people felt that *crowded venues* make confrontations more likely, and that problems are exacerbated by *irresponsible pub/club policy* (e.g. allowing too many people in, bad 'bouncing' practices, serving those who have obviously had too much to drink). Features of the town centre were also seen as playing a part: these include *lack of late-night transport, lack of late-night venues* and *poor town centre layouts* that encourage crowds in one place at the end of an evening. Restricted *licensing laws* are also held responsible for making crowding on the streets, and therefore clashes, more likely.

To illustrate how the model operates, the following are some examples of how different risk factors relating to different aspects of the social context might interact to produce disorderly outcomes:

- People barging into each other in a *crowded venue* (drinking environment) combines with *aggression* (effects of binge drinking) and the perceived obligation to *stand up for friends or self* (social/peer group norms) to encourage fighting.
- *Lack of late-night transport* (drinking environment) combines with *overconfidence* (effects of binge drinking) and the wish for *personal freedom* (attitudes and motivations) on a night out to encourage a young woman to walk home alone.
- *Friends who encourage extreme behaviour* (social/peer group norms) combines with *difficulty judging limits* (attitudes and motivations) to make a young man so drunk that it *blurs his judgement* (effects of binge drinking) – he is then encouraged by the same friends to climb a tall building.
- *Desire to push the limits* (attitudes and motivations) combines with *recklessness* (effects of binge drinking) and *lack of late-night venues* (drinking environment) to encourage a young woman to go back to a stranger's house for more drinks.

Young people and policy

With regard to the policy interventions discussed in Chapter 6, it is interesting to note that those which found most favour with the young people all addressed risk factors within the 'Drinking Environment' arm of the model. In many ways this may seem obvious or intuitive - it is arguably a lot easier for policy to have an impact on environmental factors than on individual attitudes or social norms, at least directly.

However, this may also tell us something about the attitudes of the young people. It seems that they see responsibility for the problems lying overwhelmingly with external agencies, rather than at the personal level. It may be that this reflects the association of binge drinking in the young people's minds with personal freedom and escapism – it is not a subject that they are accustomed to looking at in terms of 'responsibility' or restriction. The fact that alcohol is often viewed as an acceptable excuse for reckless behaviour, and the feeling among some young people that their age or life-stage leaves them in a position where they do not have to worry too much about responsibilities, may also be relevant here.

Many perceived campaigns aimed at raising awareness of the risks associated with binge drinking as worthwhile, and it may be that these would affect the attitudes and behaviour that surround binge drinking. Certainly the impact of drink driving adverts were noted by many of the groups, and the change in British attitudes towards drink driving since the 1960s suggests that advertising can indeed be influential in altering patterns of social behaviour. Nonetheless, the majority felt that most other forms of 'safer drinking' campaign would have only a marginal influence on their behaviour as individuals, at least in the short term. Given that some describe binge drinking as so much a habit that they cannot really think why they do it (see Chapter 3), it may be that the focus should be on "training a generation of light drinkers" as Murgraff et al., (1999) suggest - at least where the aim is reducing overall levels of binge drinking and public drunkenness.

Even if young peoples' perception that they are unlikely to be influenced by 'safer drinking' campaigns is accurate, the fact that the drinking environment has emerged as an influence on disorderly outcomes that is at least as strong as individual attitudes, social norms and the effects of binge drinking itself suggests that interventions in this area alone could prove highly effective. As Homel et al., (2001) argue, creating safer drinking environments is "primarily a 'regulatory problem', not just an 'alcohol problem'"; suitable environments can themselves affect the behaviour and attitudes of drinkers by creating expectations about what is appropriate.

Appendix A   Methodology

The available quantitative research indicates that alcohol consumption can be related to a range of social and health harms, particularly among young adults. There is also evidence to indicate that young people who indulge in 'binge drinking' are more likely to be both the perpetrators and victims of crime and disorder.

Quantitative data is valuable in this arena because it provides meaningful evidence of the *extent* of disorder in the night-time economy, for example, the number, frequency and timing of violent incidents. It can also give scientific measures of the *association* between alcohol consumption and various outcomes. With sufficiently robust samples, it produces findings that can be generalised to the whole population, and may allow reliable conclusions to be drawn about the trends in alcohol-related offending over time and the differences between relevant social or demographic groups.

However, quantitative studies linking consumption of alcohol with particular outcomes cannot give detailed information about the *social context* in which these events take place, and it is this context which needs to be understood if local and national initiatives are to be targeted effectively. Behavioural outcomes in the night-time economy are related to the social setting within which drinking and binge drinking takes place, and the social attitudes and expectations relating to this setting (see for example Graham *et al.*, 1998; Homel *et al.*, 2001; Rehm *et al.*, 1996). We can only hope to reduce undesirable outcomes by understanding how the different elements of the social context combine with drinking patterns and the effects of alcohol to produce these outcomes. It therefore becomes necessary to research young people's *interpretations* of their drinking and experiences in the night-time economy. Qualitative research is not representative and cannot be generalised to the whole population. It is usually based on a relatively small sample, and does not follow a structured question format that allows standardised comparisons between individuals. However, it is ideally suited to illuminating the context of social behaviours and the processes that underlie them. Put simply, quantitative research generally tells people what is happening, while qualitative research can illuminate *why* it is happening.

The rationale for focus groups

There are many ways to conduct qualitative research. However, the most frequently used methods involve a researcher interviewing people using an 'open' format, i.e. without the use of a structured questionnaire. Qualitative interviews can be conducted either individually or in groups. The most common format for individual interviews is the one-to-one 'depth' interview, while the most well known format for group interviews is the 'focus group' discussion.

Focus groups typically involve around six to ten participants and last between one and a half to two hours, depending on the range of issues that to be covered. The dynamics of the discussion encourage respondents to generate new ideas, stimulate debate and react to what other group members are saying. In most circumstances, the greater the homogeneity of participants, the more successful the group will be in terms of the depth of information gathered. Shared perspectives and experiences generally help the group to gel, and provide more in-depth information.

Focus groups were chosen for this study for the following reasons:

- **They are a useful qualitative tool when the objective is to generate lots of information, ranges of experience and attitudes**. The dynamics of the discussion encourage respondents to generate ideas not previously thought of, stimulate debate, or gauge reactions to what different group members might be saying. It was felt that this would be helpful in providing a depth of understanding of the issues, given that the study aimed to explore a wide range of behaviours, attitudes and experiences associated with binge drinking.
- **Focus groups are an ideal arena in which to explore the 'social construction' of knowledge and attitudes**. Through interaction and discussion between individuals, respondents form and modify their opinions in response to a given topic. This is particularly pertinent for the issue at hand, as the ultimate subject of the study is the overall 'drinking culture' among young people rather than the attitudes of specific individuals. In order to understand what is acceptable and not acceptable within this drinking culture, and to identify the common ground and differences between groups, it was necessary to establish what the shared norms are. Group discussions were considered the best tool for doing this.

It should be remembered, however, that focus groups have disadvantages as well as advantages. Key disadvantages for this study include:

- **In some cases, the group setting may restrict what respondents are prepared to reveal**. The identification of shared norms and values during a discussion may mean that people who deviate form the 'norm' in some way do not share this with the group In this study, young people may have been embarrassed to reveal more extreme drinking or offending patterns, or more sensitive experiences as a victim.
- **Focus groups allow less time to fully explore the experiences of individuals than 'one-to-one' methods**. Depth interview methodology would have been better suited to exploring drinkers' particular experiences of the night-time economy in depth – for example, by taking a specific instance of offending, risk-taking or victimhood and exploring how the situation evolved from start to finish. This may have allowed the researchers more time to challenge respondents and get behind 'top-of-mind' responses.

It is impossible to know how much these disadvantages may have influenced the research findings. However, it is worth noting the research team's *impression* that the majority of respondents did feel able to discuss the issues honestly and openly, with some admitting to quite extreme forms of behaviour. This may reflect the extent to which binge drinking among young adults, as a widespread and frequent social phenomenon, is the subject of shared cultural norms and values – one of the assumptions behind the decision to conduct focus groups in the first place.

Focus group composition

The research consisted of 16 focus group discussions with young people, carried out in 8 locations (2 groups per location). Each person interviewed was recruited directly by MORI. A matrix was drawn up to provide a representative spread by age, gender and occupational status. Further quotas were drawn up to achieve a spread of disorderly or risk-taking behaviour, and frequency of getting drunk

The plan was to recruit 10 people for each group, on the assumption that 8 would attend (standard practice in the market research industry). Due to differences in the reliability of respondents, the actual size of the focus groups ranged between 5 and 11 young people, with 123 young people participating in total.

To target young people with direct experience of a busy weekend night-time economy, the locations chosen were a mixture of market towns, large towns, cities and metropolitan areas. All young people recruited drank in a pub, bar or club at least once a month.

Subjective perceptions of frequency of drunkenness were chosen as the defining criteria of 'binge drinkers'. Groups were divided into those who reported feeling drunk at least once a week, and those who felt drunk less than once a week but at least once a month. The research found that the vast majority of these young people were drinking a great deal, very quickly, and were getting drunk as a result of 'binge drinking', whether on a weekly basis or less often. This meant that, while the young people in this study were not specifically recruited as 'binge drinkers', they did in fact display 'binge drinking' behaviour.

Ten groups were of young people who had been involved in offending or disorder after drinking during the previous year, as either perpetrator, victim or both. The majority of those in the remaining 6 groups had behaved in ways that put them 'at risk' after drinking. The three categories of experience were defined as follows:

- **'Offending' experiences:**
  - Been deliberately abusive, insulting or rude to someone.
  - Started a fight or assaulted someone else.
  - Deliberately broken/damaged/destroyed someone else's property.
  - Deliberately taken something that did not belong to you.
  - Drunk driven.

- **'Victim' experiences:**
  - Been threatened or felt intimidated by someone.
  - Been insulted or pestered by someone.
  - Been sexually harassed by someone.
  - Been assaulted or beaten up by someone.
  - Had something broken/damaged/destroyed by someone.
  - Had something stolen.

- **'At risk' experiences:**
  - Done things would not normally have done when sober.
  - Had unprotected sex after drinking alcohol.
  - Felt out of control when drunk.
  - Accepted a lift from a stranger after drinking.
  - Had a one night stand with a stranger after drinking.

Recruitment to the 'offender' and 'victim' categories was not designed to be mutually exclusive, and a key finding of the research was how often respondents had experiences as both victim and offender. In some cases, researchers found that a group recruited as 'victims' actually talked more freely about their disorderly or offending behaviour, or vice versa. Those who had been victims and/or offenders had also behaved in ways that put them 'at risk'. In addition to this, events that had happened to respondents prior to the last twelve months also frequently emerged as relevant to the discussion.

The discussions were divided equally by gender, with 4 all-male groups, 4 all-female groups, and 8 mixed groups. Groups were also evenly divided by occupational status, with 4 groups of manual workers, 4 of non-manual workers, 4 of students and 4 of non-workers. To explore any key differences between the 'late teenager' and 'early twenties' age group, it was arranged that groups should be divided into 18- to 20-year-olds and 21- to 24-year-olds, although in practice there was a slight overlap of these age boundaries within a few of the groups.

Conducting the groups

All group discussions lasted between 1½ and 2 hours, and all were moderated by a member of the MORI Project Team for the study. Respondents were encouraged to have a genuine discussion, talking between themselves rather than addressing all their remarks to the moderator. However, steps were taken to create an atmosphere of mutual trust and respect. This ensured that individuals stayed within the whole-group discussion, that the moderator could intervene to probe and move the discussion on when necessary, and that interruptions and instances of more than one person talking at a time were kept to a minimum.

To ensure consistency of approach, the four members of the project team met regularly both before and during fieldwork to discuss the format of the topic guide, the emerging findings and suggested changes in emphasis. In addition to this, six of the discussions were attended by two members of the project team, allowing one to moderate and one to take notes and reflect on the process.

In practice, the project team found that involving all four members in the fieldwork aided the process of analysis and interpretation, helping to ensure that all the relevant emerging themes were incorporated and correcting for any individual biases in approach. This process has been termed 'researcher' or 'investigator' triangulation (Denzin, 1989).

Analysis and interpretation

All 16 group discussions were tape recorded and transcribed, with the respondents' permission. The transcripts formed the 'raw data' for analysis, along with notes made by moderators during and immediately after the discussions and interviews. Researchers in the project team conducted 'brainstorming' sessions attended by all involved with the study, twice during fieldwork and once immediately afterwards. This process allowed the team to discuss the 'top-line' findings and develop key themes for the analysis.

Transcripts were analysed using a thematic indexing and charting system – a form of qualitative coding and thematic sorting often known as 'Framework'. This method involves creating an index or code frame of substantive themes and charting key findings within each theme, systematically coding up transcripts for key points and illustrative verbatim comments. Findings on the key themes for each group were then summarised on a chart incorporating the key verbatims.

The charting method ensures analysis of the data is rigorous, balanced and accurate, allowing the themes and hypotheses developed initially to be refined after a review of the evidence. Researchers were careful at all stages to look for quotes to support both sides of any given argument, rather than only those statements which appeared to support initial hypotheses.

With regard to reporting, the discussions were written up so as to provide a detailed and accurate overview of the key themes and findings. Quotes from individuals have been chosen to illustrate the range of viewpoints on each theme. Only a small minority of the quotes selected incorporate an exchange of views between two people in the group; these quotes are indicated by a plural attribute. This does not mean that discussion and debate within the focus groups did not occur, only that it should be understood as implicit. Issues which generated more lively debate are highlighted in the main body of the report. In general, when opposing viewpoints are put across for any particular point, this should be taken as indicating that the issue was a subject of disagreement and discussion within at least some of the groups.

When interpreting findings from qualitative research, it should be remembered that results are not based on quantitative statistical evidence but on a small sample of a cross-section of young people. To aid the anonymity of our respondents when quoted, each verbatim comment is identified by a person's gender, age and occupational status.

The final make-up of the focus groups can be found on the next page.

Focus group composition

Area	No. in group	Frequency of drunkenness	Risk behaviour	Actual age band	Gender composition	Occupational status
City, North of England	10	At least once a week	At risk/None	20-24	Mixed (6F,4M)	Manual worker
	11	Less often than once a week	Committed an offence	18-21	Mixed (6F,5M)	Student
Inner London	7	Less often than once a week	Victim of an offence	18-20	Mixed (5F, 2M)	Non-worker
	8	At least once a week	At risk/None	21-24	Female	Student
City, Midlands	11	At least once a week	Committed an offence	18-20	Male	Manual worker
	6	Less often than once a week	Victim of an offence	21-24	Female	Non-worker
Market Town, South East of England	7	Mixed	At risk/None	18-20	Mixed (6F,1M)	Non-worker
	5	Mixed	Committed an offence	21-24	Mixed (2F, 3M)	Manual worker
City, South West of England	6	At least once a week	Victim of an offence	21-24	Mixed (3F, 3M)	Non-manual worker
	10	Less often than once a week	At risk/None	18-20	Male	Non-manual worker
Greater London	6	Less often than once a week	Committed an offence	18-21	Female	Non-manual worker
	7	At least once a week	Victim of an offence	18-21	Male	Student
Large Town, Wales	8	At least once a week	At risk/None	18-20	Mixed (3F,5M)	Student
	6	Mixed	Committed an offence	21-24	Male	Non-worker
Large Town, Midlands	7	Mixed	Victim of an offence	18-20	Female	Manual worker
	8	At least once a week	At risk/None	20-25*	Mixed (4F,4M)	Non-manual worker

*The 25-year-old in the group had a birthday between recruitment and the focus group being held.

References

Aitken, P. (1985) An observational study of young adults' drinking groups – II. Drink purchasing procedures, group pressures and alcohol consumption by companions as predictors of alcohol consumption, *Alcohol and Alcoholism*, Vol. 20, No. 4., pp. 445-457.

Brown, S., Goldman, M., Inn, A. and Anderson, L. (1980) Expectations of reinforcement from alcohol: their domain and relation to drinking patterns, *Journal of Consulting and Clinical Psychology*, Vol. 48, pp. 419-426.

Budd, T., and Sims, L. (2001) *Antisocial behaviour and disorder: findings from the 2000 British Crime Survey*, Findings, No. 145. London: Home Office.

Cookson, H. (1992) Alcohol use and offence type in young offenders, *British Journal of Criminology*, Vol.32, No. 3, pp. 352-360.

Deehan, A. (1999) *Alcohol and Crime: Taking Stock*, Crime Reduction Research Series Paper 3. London: Home Office.

Deehan, A., Marshall, E., Saville, E. (2002) *Drunks and Disorder: Processing intoxicated arrestees in two city-centre custody suites*, Police Research Series Paper 150. London: Home Office.

Denzin, N. (1989) *The Research Act* (3rd edn). Englewood Cliffs, New Jersey: Prentice-Hall.

Gilbert, M. J. (1990) The Anthropologist as Alcohologist: Qualitative Perspectives and Methods in Alcohol Research, *International Journal of the Addictions*, Vol 25, No. 2, pp. 127-143.

Graham, K., Leonard, K., Room, R., Wild, C., Pihl, R., Bois, C., and Single, E. (1998) Current directions in research on understanding and preventing intoxicated aggression, *Addiction*, Vol. 93, No. 5, pp. 659-676.

Harnett, R., Thom, B., Herring, R., and Kelly, M. (2000) Alcohol in Transition: Towards a Model of Young Men's Drinking Styles, *Journal of Youth Studies*, Vol. 3, No. 1, pp. 61-77.

Homel, R., McIlwain, G., and Carvolth, R. (2001) Creating Safer Drinking Environments, *International Handbook of Alcohol Dependence and Problems*, Chapter 37, pp. 721-737. Edited by Heather, N., Peters, T.J., and Stockwell, T. Chichester: John Wiley & Sons Ltd.

Honess, T., Seymour, L. and Webster, R. (2000) *The social contexts of underage drinking*. London: Home Office.

Jeffs, W. and Saunders, W. (1983) 'Minimising alcohol-related offences by enforcement of the existing licensing legislation', *British Journal of Addiction*, Vol. 78, pp. 66-77.

Marsh, P. and Kibby, K. (1992) *Drinking and Public Disorder*. Oxford: Alden Press.

Mattinson, J. (2001) *Stranger and Acquaintance Violence: Practice Messages from the British Crime Survey*, Briefing Note 7/01. London: Home Office.

Measham, F. (1996) The 'big bang' approach to sessional drinking: changing patterns of alcohol consumption amongst young people in north west England. *Addiction Research*, Vol 4, pp283-299.

Midanik, L. (1999) Drunkenness, feeling the effects and 5+ measures, *Addiction*, Vol. 94, No. 6, pp. 887-897.

Moore, L., Smith, C., and Catford, J. (1994) Binge drinking: prevalence, patterns and policy, *Health Education Research*, Vol. 9, No. 4, pp. 497-505.

Murgraff, V., Parrott, A. and Bennett, P. (1999) Risky Single-Occasion Drinking among young people – Definition, correlates, policy and intervention: A broad overview of the research findings, *Alcohol and Alcoholism*, Vol. 34, No. 1, pp. 3-14.

Newburn, T. and Shiner, M. (2001) *Teenage Kicks? Young people and alcohol: A review of the literature*. Joseph Rowntree Foundation.

Norton, A. (1998) Alcohol-related crime: The good practice of the magistrates courts, *Alcohol and Alcoholism*, Vol. 33, No. 1, pp.78-82.

Ramsay, M. (1982) *City Centre Crime; a Situational Approach to Prevention*, Research and Planning Unit Paper 19. London: Home Office.

Rehm, J., Ashley, M.J., Room, R., Single, E., Bondy, S., Ferrence, R. and Giesbrecht, N. (1996) On the emerging paradigm of drinking patterns and their social and health consequences, *Addiction*, Vol. 91, No. 11, pp. 1615-1621

Richardson, A. and Budd, T. (2003) *Alcohol, crime and disorder: a study of young adults.* London: Home Office.

Russ, N. and Geller, E. (1987) Training bar personnel to prevent drunken driving: a field evaluation, *American Journal of Public Health*, Vol. 77, pp. 952-954.

Shepherd, J. and Brickley, M. (1996) The relationship between alcohol intoxication, stressors and injury in urban violence, British Journal of Criminology, Vol. 36, No. 4, pp. 546-566.

Shepherd, J., Shapland, M., Pearce, N. and Scully, C. (1990) Pattern, severity and aetiology of injuries in victims of assault, *Journal of the Royal Society of Medicine*, Vol. 83, No. 2, pp. 75-78.

Turning Point (1998) *An Evaluation of the Geelong Local Industry Accord.* Victoria: Alcohol and Drug Centre Inc.

Webb, E., Ashton, C., Kelly, P. and Kamali, F. (1996) Alcohol and drug use in U.K. university students, *The Lancet*, Vol. 348, pp. 922-925.

Wells, S., Graham, K. and West, P. (1998) The good, the bad and the ugly: Responses by security staff to aggressive incidents in public drinking settings, *Journal of Drug Issues*, Canada: Addiction Research Foundation.

RDS Publications

Requests for Publications

Copies of our publications and a list of those currently available may be obtained from:

> Home Office
> Research, Development and Statistics Directorate
> Communication Development Unit
> Room 275, Home Office
> 50 Queen Anne's Gate
> London SW1H 9AT
> Telephone: 020 7273 2084 (answerphone outside of office hours)
> Facsimile: 020 7222 0211
> E-mail: publications.rds@homeoffice.gsi.gov.uk

alternatively

why not visit the RDS web-site at
>   Internet: http://www.homeoffice.gov.uk/rds/index.htm

where many of our publications are available to be read on screen or downloaded for printing.